REFLECTIONS
OF OLD CORNWALL

REFLECTIONS OF OLD CORNWALL

A FURTHER SELECTION OF HISTORIC PHOTOGRAPHS
FROM THE REG WATKISS ARCHIVE

Compiled and Written by
Reg Watkiss

HALSGROVE

First published in Great Britain in 2005
Reprinted 2009 and 2015

British Library Cataloguing-in-Publication Data
A CIP record for this title is available from the British Library

ISBN 978 1 84114 441 2

HALSGROVE
Halsgrove House,
Ryelands Business Park,
Bagley Road, Wellington, Somerset TA21 9PZ
Tel: 01823 653777   Fax: 01823 216796
email: sales@halsgrove.com

Part of the Halsgrove group of companies
Information on all Halsgrove titles is available at: www.halsgrove.com

Printed and bound in China by Everbest Printing Co Ltd

CONTENTS

INTRODUCTION

This book brings together the second collection of photographic prints I have compiled for the publishers, Halsgrove, from my extensive personal archive, the results of almost half a century of collecting images of Cornwall. It includes the work of professional photographers, amateur enthusiasts, and also the efforts of the inspired, or perhaps lucky, snapshot cameramen. The selection covers the mid-Victorian beginnings of photography and continues throughout the following century and into the 1940s. *Lost Cornwall,* the first of these books, presented the viewer with images from the very dawn of Fox Talbot's invention, introduced in 1840, and there are further examples in this new book dating to within a decade or so of that era.

From my first introduction, one afternoon in the early 1960s, to a very beautiful collection of Victorian photographs belonging to the painter Alathea Garstin, I was hooked on an interest that was to be a lasting one. And only a week before writing this Introduction my enthusiasm was again rekindled on discovering a fine print of a street scene in Wadebridge, which has become a late contender for inclusion here

It was good to have a second invitation from Simon Butler the publisher, since the necessary process of selection for my first book meant that I could include only part of the large number of original prints, glass plates, sheet film, and copy negatives that form the collection. I had to reject many of excellent quality and interest in order to keep the presentation within the limits then established for the first publication. There is still, as previously, a dominance of photographs from the west and south-west of the county, since the many years I have lived in West Penwith have obviously presented the chances to acquire larger numbers of collectable examples from this locality. It is true also that the greater concentration of professional photographers was to be found in the far west, which was then, as it still is today, more densely populated. However, I am pleased that coverage of the upper easterly and northern reaches is more evident this time, helped by the quite extensive trips I have made in the last two years to these areas searching for photographs, plus the keen assistance from other enthusiasts and friends who have come up with interesting examples and finds.

In the last few years quite a few engaging publications have appeared devoted often to exploring in detail just one small area or village, a number of them promoted by my publishers Halsgrove through their Community History Series, adding greatly to the ever-growing general and historical knowledge of Cornwall. My approach differs from these in that it begins with finding the photograph, assessing its quality and technical excellence, perhaps noting it as a fine example of the photographers' craft or the rarity of its subject matter, to mention just a few of the reasons that provoke my interest, with the caption then added as support for the image. For example, quite often I have found splendid prints about which little or nothing is known, such the photograph of Wadebridge (see the section on transport), in which appears an overloaded conveyance waiting outside the Commercial Hotel.

Others images have had their content further enhanced only after a chance discovery or meeting: the photograph of Penzance promenade beach showing the wheeled bathing huts, provided for the protection of the Victorian lady bathers' modesty, being just one of these. The exposure, made in the late 1870s or early 1880s, I took into a local Penzance inn some 35 years ago to show to the landlord, and was informed by a wiry ninety-seven-year-old customer, comfortably seated with his pint of beer in a corner settle, that he had helped his grandfather who was in charge of these bathing machines, all those years ago, to lead the donkey who pulled them up and down to the water's edge. Perhaps a detail of little historical importance some would say, but for me it helps bring to life the whole picture. This was just one of the many like occurrences with its warm social incidence, that has promoted my continued enthusiasm and fun over the years.

I make no claim to being an historian, and so the supporting captions to each picture are often based on information gathered just as described. Who better to rely on than those who have a direct connection to the subjects depicted, or who have through accounts of things handed down through the family and community, direct access to detailed stories of events stretching back into the past. I have always double- and treble-checked information given, and referred to specialists in any particular field of activity where necessary. However, in providing information it is impossible to completely avoid errors and just a very few small ones were fairly quickly picked up after the publication of *Lost Cornwall*, corrected now in the reprint. That said, as I indicated then, the brief historical information given here is meant to be used with confidence for reference purposes.

Whilst some photographs demand supporting information in order to make them come alive, others impress and engage our interest and give up their secrets purely by the power of their image. A great photograph often says it all and transcends the passage of time, just as a great painting or other work of art.

As I worked through the last winter months of 2004 on the prints for this presentation, racking up and down the large old wall-mounted plate-size enlarger in my 'wet darkroom' (the reference term now dominant which distinguishes the gungy photographic-film processing workshop from that refined space used for the digitally captured computer image), I was suddenly very conscious of being in at the end of an era and myself acting out a part in photographic history. Days spent in the red safelight gloom, permeated with the cocktail of chemical smells from caustic developers and acid fixers, cold running water further agitating the arthritis in my hands. I several times regretted turning down the publisher's offer to scan everything from my original plates, prints and copy negatives, doubting perhaps those who would have interpreted that torn and faded sepia print, or damaged plate, at least as I felt it should look. Secretly of course I know they would have dealt with things perfectly well using their new-fangled high-tech equipment. There we have it! As I have processed the images I can assure the purist that for my part there are no digitally added bits or lines or other details. The only alterations to the content of the prints are those made during the copy negative and enlarging exposure to enhance the contrast of some faded originals, perhaps to remove the occasional crack or harsh blemish of a damaged plate. In most cases the whole of the image, as the author of the work first published it, is presented.

I suppose I like to muse on the fact that if this archive presentation is among the last of those productions appearing at the possible twilight and passing of the photographic image as we have known it for almost a century and a half, accomplished by traditional methods, the latent image trapped in silver halide coated film and paper, then coaxed into the light and life of day from a dungeon-like room reeking of chemicals, it may have just that something that adds a special and collectable aspect to its production. Call it my homage to all the photographers and past participants of the art form who have left us this legacy of images from Cornwall.

Reg Watkiss
Penzance 2005

ACKNOWLEDGEMENTS

I acknowledge first the names of the photographers whose work can be positively identified and which forms part of my collection, along with prints and original plates from photographers who can be identified through the subject style and quality of their work. There are however quite a large percentage of fine prints included here, work by both obvious professionals and others, whose names are now lost. Presented alphabetically, not in order of importance, the known photographers are: W.J. Bennett of Camborne and Hayle, brothers William and Joseph Broad of Bodmin and Wadebridge, J.C. Burrow ARPS of Camborne, Charles Roberts Chapple of St Levan, Francis Frith, John Gibson, Herbert Gibson and Alexander Gibson of the Lyonesse Studio Scilly and of Penzance, Govier of Truro, Redruth and St Buryan, Charles Napier Hemy RA RWS and daughters, W.M. Harrison of Falmouth and Helston, Humphreys of St Ives, Arthur James of Bodmin, Moody of Penzance, Daphne Pearson of St Ives, Harry Penhaul of Penzance, Robert Preston of Penzance, R.M. Reynolds of Torpoint, H. Roberts of Mevagissey, Richards Brothers of Penzance, Edwin Trembath of St-Just-in-Penwith, and the gifted amateur William Thomas also of that town. The Thorn family of professional photographers in Bude complete the list of known photographers.

Once again I have to pay tribute to the important contributions made to my collection almost four decades ago by Pat Pilkerton of Newlyn, and Tony Pawlyn, then of Newlyn, now Head Librarian of Falmouth Maritime Museum, the late Dr Godfrey Symonds of Penzance (and more recently his son Adrian Symonds), and within the last decade the grandson of the photographer J.C. Burrow RPS, the late George Burrow, formerly of Hayle, and his son John Burrow of Goldsithney

Two friends, both local history enthusiasts, have as on previous occasions, been of great help: Clive Carter, author of a number of books on Cornwall, has been ever-willing to assist authentication on some point, or to verify a story surrounding an event, in particular those relating to shipping and mining, whilst Michael Eddy an enthusiastic and well-informed photographic and postcard collector himself, has been generous in his attempts to flush out photographs for me in those areas not so well represented in my collection. Henry and Alison Symons of St Ives have greatly assisted me in putting together the section dealing with that fishing town, allowing me to add examples from their collection and supporting them with their lifetime of local knowledge. Margaret Powel of Lamorna, a granddaughter of the painter Charles Napier Hemy RA RWS, allowed me to take home the entire box-load of family photographic albums she had inherited, from which I extracted the prints which make up the section given over to Falmouth Town.

All the following people have given help, provided valuable information, or in some way added to my collection and thus to the contents of this book. They are again listed in alphabetical order: Norman Ampleford of Penzance; Cedric Appleby, local historian and former lecturer; Alan Austin, collectables dealer; John Chope formerly of Sennen lifeboat; Rubina Craze of Zennor; Paul Dyer of the Copperhouse Gallery and Bookshop, Hayle; Stan Harris, former Western Region locomotive driver and prior to that stoker of the crack 'Cornishman Express' steam locomotive; Pat Laimbeer former professional photographer; Ray Marks, fishermen; Alan Nudd fishing boat skipper; Tony Paling former Cable & Wireless engineer, John Ralph of Porthgwarra; Phillip Rowe transport archivist; Sue Shapland, postcard collector; John Smith from St Austell formerly Head of Photography at St Austell College; John Smith from Penzance, postcard dealer; Paul Thomas, railway works engineer and fitter; Mrs L. Tredinnick (the bride seen in the charming wedding photograph she loaned to me); Liz Trenary of Sennen who came up with some extraordinary aviation photographs; Alan Uren of Newlyn for his observations on his home town.

A general thanks also to the many others over the past that have shown an interest and given me their help.

These representatives, both past and present, of various organisations and institutions have also been most helpful: Mike Cotton, twice formally Mayor of Penzance, was able to assist with the checking of various Penzance town records; Master Mariner, Captain Phil Moran, Operations Manager of St Ives Lifeboat was a helpful contact regarding details of that service; Phil Westren Penance Pirates Rugby Club historian and archivist was able to assist from his records regarding the photograph of the early activities of the team, and also with details relating to the photograph of the old workhouse at Madron in the village where he lives. Alison Bevan, Curator of Penlee House Museum and Art Gallery, was once again very helpful when approached, whilst the staff of both Penzance libraries, the Morrab Private Library and the Town Library assisted in a number of very useful ways whenever approached.

PENZANCE

Market Jew Street, Penzance, 1871

This finely detailed, early topographical photograph of the main street in Penzance, was my immediate choice to begin this collection, for it has all the style and quality seen in the work of one of the best of early Cornish and Penzance photographers, Robert Preston. When I first discovered it some thirty-five years ago, amongst a group of prints marked Francis Frith photographs, I at first accepted that labelling. The experience I've gained over the years since however confidently allows me now to acknowledge it as Preston's work. He had in fact, in 1870, moved from his Penzance Esplanade premises up to 23 The Terrace, Market Jew Street, a short distance across the road from where the camera has been set up. It is 7.18am as shown by the clock on the Market House and it would for obvious reasons have been easy for him to be up and out early, taking advantage of the stillness in the street at this time of day. Any photographer, wanting to record clearly the architecture and general detail of the scene with only the slow wet plates then available would have chosen this hour to avoid unwanted movement affecting sharpness throughout the extended shutter speed required. However, as can be seen by the ghost image on the left-hand pavement, just below Fox's Prince Of Wales Inn, someone managed to walk through the camera's field of view during the exposure. The Humphry Davy statue, celebrating the life of the great Penzance inventor and scientist, has been a prominent feature at the top of Market Jew Street for over a century and a quarter now, but is missing in this photograph. It was erected in front of the Market House one year after this photograph was taken, in 1872, with an unveiling ceremony on 17 October that year.

Alverton Street, Penzance c.1870

In this photograph, taken from the west side of the Market House (known at this time, prior to the completion of St John's Hall, as the Guild Hall), everyone obligingly stands still in Alverton Street so that the Gibsons could achieve a clear yet animated representation of the contemporary Victorian scene. I say everyone, with one exception, as in the previous early view, for this time a young man obviously thought he was beyond the viewing eye of the camera as he walked past, causing the blurred image we can see extreme right. This again tells us that a slow wet plate was in use and the exposure was therefore probably made before the introduction of the faster dry plates of 1878. The trees on the left, behind the railings and wall, are in the front garden of Alverne House, a very fine property which the successful photographer, Robert Preston, purchased in 1881. A print of the Preston family and friends playing croquet in the garden at the rear of the house, is to be seen on page 30.

Market Place, Penzance, late nineteenth century

Once again, as seen in the previous Alverton Street scene, everyone seems quite happy to play their part in making the photograph by posing to a command, and this is a feature of many street scenes one views from this period. Imagine trying to organize such an event at this present time, particularly as many people dodge for cover immediately they see a camera pointing remotely in their direction. The bow-windowed shop frontage on the left was Chudleigh's Eating House. The exterior appears to be constructed of a warm oak, inviting the market dealers of the time into a comfortable interior with settles and dark mahogany bench tables on which to dine and discuss the day's business.

Shakerley's Corner, Penzance, late nineteenth century

Viewed here from the top side of Market Place, the location was generally referred to in the late nineteenth century by the name of the chemist and druggist we see. Looking past the townspeople towards the Green Market, a large shop wall clock on Rossiters lets us know once again that this is an early morning job for the photographer, its 8am and summer sunlight from the southeast is illuminating the open street.

Causewayhead, 1880s

Causewayhead was and still is a street with much character. It has throughout several centuries provided the interest and facilities of a diversity of small shops, eating venues and places of entertainment, with a good selection of inns, though there are today fewer of such hostelries than existed in Victorian times. Parsons' the grocers are occupying No.13 but moved to No.1 by the end of 1887, after which the name was removed from the side wall of the shop we see on the right, so this photograph was made sometime prior to that, in the 1880s. Stewart's, the general ironmongers, shown here trading at Nos 7 and 8, continued in business at various sites in the town for over one hundred and thirty years.

The Duke of Cumberland, Causewayhead, 1897

This once well-appointed inn is seen here decorated to celebrate the Diamond Jubilee of Queen Victoria in 1897. Parts of the courtyard and frontage can still be seen leading off from an opening beside No.70 Causewayhead. The posters let us know that horse-drawn vehicles such as dog carts, Victorias, phaetons, as well as saddle horses and ponies were available for hire, which would have meant that good stables were a feature of this posting establishment.

Chapel Street, 1890s

This is a street with both architectural and much historical interest. It is of late Victorian date and shows, top right the Egyptian House, with its quite unique façade constructed on the site an earlier Regency building in 1836. Then, located top left under the flagpole and the magnificent Victorian lamp, is the Union Hotel which has records and history reaching back into the early sixteenth century. Below this, also sporting a flagpole, and once advertised as the Largest Temperance Hotel in Cornwall, is The Regent. At the bottom of the road, overlooking the sea, is the parish church of St Mary, erected in 1834 on the site of an old chapel. In a cottage-style town house, situated close by the church, Maria Branwell lived when a young girl, prior to her marriage and becoming mother of the Bronte's of literary fame.

Viewing Mount's Bay today from the raised vantage point of St Mary's open churchyard can lead to the impression that one is tapping into a Victorian time capsule, particularly on those days when the sea is host to the many small sailing craft and fishing boats that still use these waters. Even today the scene evokes the nostalgia represented in topographical lithographic prints, hand-coloured engravings or sepia-toned photographic panoramas of the nineteenth century.

The Union Hotel, Chapel Street c.1880

This old and established posting hotel has much history surrounding it, but it is particularly known for its connection with an event relating to the first news to reach English shores of Nelson's victory at Trafalgar on the 21 October 1805. A signal taken by a Mount's Bay fishing lugger from a returning warship, HMS *Pickle*, in the second week of the November following, gave a report of his success and this was subsequently relayed ashore where it was announced to a gathered audience in the Union Hotel from either the assembly room, or the ancient theatre. There has in recent times been some question as to which of these it was but both are of much local interest. The theatre, only parts of which now survive, is said to be the second oldest in Britain. The assembly room is now used as a ballroom. This private coach with its four-in-hand seen waiting here may well have been one of the facilities advertised by the Hotel as available to guests for posting and excursions into the surrounding countryside. In this photograph it has a rather formal air that leads one to feel it depicts a special occasion. The photographic technique dates it as being made in either the late 1870s, or early 1880s. The Longhurst's were proprietors of the Union during the years 1867 to 1887.

This year of 2005 as I write, marks the bicentenary of Lord Nelson's final sea victory and death during the great battle.

The Terrace, Market Jew Street, Penzance

Horse buses wait below the terrace in the early afternoon Victorian sunlight of Market Jew Street. The Penzance to Camborne Bus stands directly beneath Gibsons the photographers who moved up to the site seen here, next to Bolithos Bank, in 1879. They had previously rented rooms on the promenade, where they had been housed in part of the old Royal Promenade Baths which was to be demolished soon after in 1883. Most of the horses for these vehicles would be held and fed during the waiting periods throughout the day in stables belonging to Fox's Prince Of Wales Inn, which was just opposite across the road.

Penzance Harbour, 1869

From a high vantage point a short distance north-east of Abbey Slip, Robert Preston made this photograph of Penzance Harbour as it was in 1869. The enlargement I have made here which is presented along with the full view provided by the original print, helps us to see more clearly the several fine sailing craft and a paddle steamer berthed there at the time. The packet paddle boat is the SS *Earl of Arran*. She was used to carry cargoes and people between Penzance and the Scilly Isles and shared this mainland linking service with another screw-driven steam ship, the *Little Western*. In 1872 both got into difficulties and were wrecked.

Penzance Old Harbour, 1860s

This print dates from the 1860s as far as can be established and certainly from before 1869 when one compares it with certain other positively dated prints of that year. Two are shown in my previous book *Lost Cornwall* (on pages 13 and 19) and feature broad views of the harbour and the Abbey Slip. In the 1870s view of the area, large letters across the façades of the centre quayside buildings are clearly shown advertising the existence of the Steam Saw Mills working on the site at that date, and these are just visible also on the left of the 1869 harbour scene. By the 1870s several new buildings have been added to the scene. Prior to the completion of the floating dock in 1884, vessels sailed right in and up to the small quays and jetty's, discharging cargoes or taking them on. Coulsons Granary was located next to the Abbey Slip and this imposing granite structure which was such a feature of the view then, is still there, though at the present time in a rather sad state of neglect and decay.

St Mary's Church which overlooks the scene like a sentinel, built in 1834, was created the parish church of Penzance out of Madron in 1871.

South Quay, Penzance 1870s

One can almost hear seabird cries, the creaking of masts, wind flapping canvas and savour the cocktail of quayside smells of rope and tar, tallow and sea-soaked hulls, whilst viewing this wonderfully composed photograph. It evokes so well the atmosphere of this very busy port in the days of sail. From several detailed clues it is possible to suggest the exposure was made around the middle of the 1870s and before construction began on the floating dock in 1879, which had an opening ceremony in November 1884. The coastal schooners, brigantines, sailing trawlers and other small working boats that used Penzance prior to the wet dock being put into service would be seen, as here, lying up between tides on the harbour mud. St Mary's church establishes an imposing and stabilizing vertical in the composition.

Late Victorian Dockside Scene

With the opening of the floating dock in 1884, larger vessels, such as this passenger sailing ship, were able to use the port. Posters on the walls of the dockside Dolphin Tavern throughout much of the Victorian era advertised passage to New York and other parts of the United States. Many tin miners took up the offer to go to America in the 1880s and 1890s following the failure and closure of a large number of Cornish mines due to the collapse in the price of tin.

Unloading Timber, Penzance Dock, late nineteenth century

This is one of the numerous Norwegian ships which came loaded with timber for use in the Cornish tin mines throughout much of the nineteenth century. The two balls seen in the distance, centre right, were used for signalling to ships the depth of water at the harbour mouth.

East Coast Fishing Boats, Penzance Dock, 1890s

Although Newlyn harbour has been the centre for the fishing in West Penwith over several centuries now, being situated approximately one mile south-west of Penzance which has mostly had a commercial shipping history. On this occasion it looks as if the whole of the Lowestoft fleet of sailing trawlers working the locality decided to berth in the Penzance dock. One reason for bringing them all in here together could have been bad weather in the fishing grounds off Mount's Bay, in which case Newlyn would have been packed with local fishing boats using the home port for shelter.

Mediterranean Bound

At the height of the pilchard fishing industry in Cornwall, this would have been a common site at the Penzance dock and at certain other harbours throughout the county. Processed pilchards, salted down in special tanks and finally pressed into the wooden casks we see here, were exported widely to the Mediterranean countries, particularly Italy. 'Fair Maids' was a local name often applied to the fish, the sparkle of their silver undersides, gleaming in the clear turbulent water as the seine net circled and enclosed a large shoal, gave rise to this colourful description.

Church Street 1890s

Just across the road from the previously pictured dock scene, this street provided the sailor and harbour workers with a choice of three inns. The Ship Inn just below the church, the Dock Hotel located where the two people stand, and out of sight left, below the post office and a ships' chandler, The Dolphin. The Dolphin and the Dock are still there but the Ship Inn has long since gone. The following print features the same area as depicted in a work by an early Newlyn School painter, A. Stanhope Forbes.

Christmas Eve, 1897

Stanhope Forbes the Newlyn School artist kept a black and white photographic record of much of his work and in the 1970s I was offered the chance to make a negative record of all the whole plate photographs mounted in an album. Although this is not a direct photograph from life, I felt it was appropriate to include it alongside the previous print as it brings the scene to life in such a moving way – one can almost hear the strains of the Christmas carol echoing through the gathering dusk all those years ago.

There was no indication as to who had carried out the photography for him over the years but it could have been the work of more than one of the Penzance photographers since there is evidence in the original prints of a variation in style, and sometimes quality of detail and sharpness.

Humphry Davy (1778–1829), Penzance Centenary Ceremony, 1929

This gathering of townspeople and local dignitaries assembled before the Humphry Davy monument on 8 June 1929 were celebrating the life of this locally and nationally esteemed inventor and scientist in the centenary year of his death. The two men seen placing a wreath are John Symons, President of The Royal Geological Society, and John Coulson Tregarthen, President of The Royal Institution of Cornwall. The Mayor of Penzance, Councillor W. G. Goodfellow stands just behind and to the right of them, whilst two Sergeants-at-Mace can be made out clearly on either side, in amongst the crowd in their ceremonial regalia.

One of the several photographers sent to cover the ceremony by the *Western Morning News* is kneeling on the draped roof of the Taximen's rest hut, peering into the hood of what looks to be a quarter-plate reflex camera to record the event. The photograph featured here was taken by another of them. Of interest also is the inclusion in the picture (top right) of the studio and shop frontage of Robert Preston, the photographer referred to in the first caption in this book. Preston had moved from No.23, on the Terrace, Market Jew Street, to this location at No.40 Market Street in 1885, and continued the business there for the rest of his life until 1932. Born in 1838, his very successful career had continued until just a year before his death on 29 January 1933 at the age of ninety four, and it is claimed that as old as he was, he continued to take the occasional studio portrait.

St Michael's Mount

This is the view of St Michael's Mount from the mainland, the name of the island having origins linking it with the priory established here in ancient times. A tidal causeway allows walking access at low tide, otherwise a short boat trip from Marazion is necessary. It has much history surrounding it, the first reference to it being in a document of AD495, and it receives a mention in the Domesday book. It provided the first port in the area known as Mount's Bay, which of course derives its name from the island. Much written about, painted, photographed as here, this shows it prior to the planting of the trees in the 1870s when fairly extensive building additions were made. The masts of a sailing ship can just be made out behind the harbour wall.

Mount's Bay, 1911

The following four photographs have been chosen to show two major happenings in Mount's Bay during just one year. It would however be possible to fill the pages of an extensive publication with data and supporting photographic illustrations covering the many and varied events that have made up the life of the Bay, and which have presented the people of the immediate area with newsworthy, often highly dramatic spectacles since the established invention of photography in 1839.

Eastern Beach July 1911

Schools of pilot whales have, I am told on the good authority of fishermen and others with local marine knowledge, always been a feature of the seas around West Cornwall and have at times be known to beach themselves, with sad consequences as shown here. On this occasion however the number of stranded creatures was so great that thousands turned up to view them. Efforts were made to get them back into the swim but it was to no avail. They arrived on 1 July and these two photographs, along with the very many others that were made covering the event, would have been taken quite soon after. It's unlikely that the sightseers would have been standing so close within a short time during the summer week, since it is also recorded that the decomposing carcasses soon presented a dreadful stench.

The *Salutto*, Mount's Bay, 13 December 1911

This Norwegian barque was to become a total wreck after her Master, in appalling visibility on 13 December 1911, mistook the Land's End headland for Lizard Point. She was driven ashore in Mount's Bay in the teeth of the south-westerly gale and heavy seas, just east of St Michael's Mount, off Perranuthnoe. She was in ballast at the time, bound for South America. Fortunately all hands were saved by the crew of the Penzance lifeboat, the *Elizabeth And Blanche*, whose Coxswain T. E. Vingoe had directed the courageous and dangerous rescue, the vessel being within half a mile of the shore when the men were taken off. The rescued seamen then double-banked the oars to assist clearing the stricken vessel so that the lifeboat's sail could be set for the passage back to Newlyn. The *Salutto* was to join the many other vessels that had come to grief over the centuries in the often changing and dramatic weather conditions of Mount's Bay.

Gathering Seaweed, Mount's Bay

The gathering up of seaweed deposited on beaches, driven onshore by winds and heavy sea swell after a storm, was once a common site around many Cornish beaches adjacent to good growing farmland, such as that found in the vicinity of Mount's Bay. Providing it was not over used, seaweed provided an excellent fertiliser on local soils.

View Over Penzance

This view over the town looks south-west across the railway station and harbour from fields soon to be built on. The old Coastguard Station complex is clearly seen on the left-hand side.

The End of the Boer War

As far as I can establish, this is the parade that took place marking the end of the Boer War in 1902 and was photographed from an upstairs window of a house at the top of Morrab Road, Penzance. The banner hanging on what is now the Public Library, reads (as fully disclosed on another photograph in my collection), 'The Path of Duty is the Road to Glory'. One consequence of this sobering Victorian-twilight prediction, leads on to the next print included here.

The South African War Memorial

This is as the Boer War is titled on the memorial erected in the Morrab Gardens in remembrance of the eight local men who lost their lives in this bitter conflict; first dedicated here in a ceremony in 1904.

Newlyn RFC versus Penzance RFC, 1938

In 1938 Newlyn Town rugby team and visiting local rivals Penzance changed into their playing kit in the Fishermen's Mission and together walked the mile or so up the Newlyn Combe valley, thence to climb the hill to the home side's St Goulder pitch, on the left as you approach Tredavoe village. All this was prior to setting about each other with that special enthusiasm and resolve a local derby game inspires, as is so fully conveyed in this excellent action photograph. Such conditions might well put some of our modern thoroughbred players off their game. They then had to walk all the way back to Newlyn after the final whistle, to wash off the grime before changing.

The advent of the Second World War saw the end of regular rugby games as such this, but with the war's end in 1945 the amalgamation of the two teams brought about the Newlyn and Penzance RFC – the Penzance Pirates as they were then named. Since then on the club has grown in stature and have become recognised throughout the country for their achievements. Recent restructuring has meant taking up a more central role in county rugby by establishing the team base and ground in Truro, adopting the name the Cornish Pirates.

Robert Preston and Family, 1907

I began this Penzance section with a Robert Preston photograph and it seemed so appropriate to end with another, this charming study of family and friends gathered together in the garden of his Penzance residence, Alverton House, on the 30 March, 1907.

TWO FISHING TOWNS
NEWLYN AND ST IVES

Throughout the nineteenth century and into the twentieth, fishing in Cornwall grew and flourished at ports and coastal villages around the whole of its coastline. In many a remote cove it would often provide the needs of the whole community. In the main towns and larger fishing villages the industry was developed in ways that created new work and improvements in general living standards. The export by sea of dried, salted, processed fish was established, whilst the arrival of the railways brought fresh fish markets in major cities at once within a few hours' reach, further promoting growth. My choice of the photographs here, of just two of these fishing towns, reflects the fact that my collection of Newlyn and St Ives images is particularly comprehensive, whilst they serve to illustrate the activities which went on county-wide. Even so, I am mindful of the local and regional differences affecting the characteristics of the boats and working methods that existed in the county and, where possible, I have included photographs elsewhere in these pages to demonstrate this. The twentieth century has seen a gradual erosion of the fishing traditions of Cornwall but, fall outside the approximately hundred year period covered in this book.

Newlyn Town c.1880

This view over Newlyn looking south-west across the town has been difficult to date precisely. It was we know taken prior to 1885 but obviously some years after 1868 as St Peter's Church (shown bottom right) is here well established. Work on the building, which is dedicated to the patron saint of fishermen, began in 1868. Centre top can be seen the old harbour, but as yet there is no sign of the south pier. The foundation stone for this much-needed addition to the town's fishing industry was laid on 29 June 1885. It was however most certainly once part of an outcrop on the hill immediately above the church known locally as the 'Devils Rock', associated in legend with the devil, and so called because of what appears to be a claw-like imprint incised in the granite. At one time, I'm told, local children played on and around it with little regard for life and limb, ignoring of course their parents' chiding and warnings of the dangers. I have listened to hair-raising stories regarding these activities.

I recently climbed the hill road for the purpose of checking out the photograph and it was a struggle to get near the 'Devil's Rock', though I eventually did, through overgrown briers and dense undergrowth. Gone are the children's shrill cries and taunting laughter that once filled the summer days, as devilment provoked the boys and girls into perilously swinging from an overhanging tree, or balancing upside down from the rock on the very edge of the lofty drop. Today, deserted by the children and probably the devil also, one still looks out from this vantage point over the town which, though swelled by additional dwellings and developments over a century, still retains much the same shape and character. Viewing the church below one couldn't help reflecting that St Peter not only acted as a guardian for the fishermen but also put in some overtime on the children's behalf who seem to have made it unscathed despite all the lurid stories I listened to.

Gwavas Lake, Newlyn, 1870s

The young girl seen here is standing on 'Green Slip', as she views the Newlyn lugger fleet setting off for the fishing grounds. The South Pier was yet to be constructed at this location starting in 1885, so this view of the bay flanking the south end of Newlyn's foreshore known as 'Gwavas Lake' was taken sometime in the decade before that; looking at the photographic quality for a clue, probably the late 1870s.

Fish Jowsters, Newlyn c.1880

Referred to locally as both 'Quay Alley' and 'Keel Alley', the first of these names denotes that this stretch of stony beach backs on to the old harbour wall, whilst the second has origins associated with the laying down of keels that once took place in a boatbuilder's yard close by. The fish jowsters (hawkers of fish) are of course awaiting the return of the boats with their catch but it does look as if they are in for quite a wait since there isn't a fishing vessel in sight, and the tide is well out. However, In this wonderfully relaxed photographic image of the late 1870s or early 1880s we can contemplate with them both the telling foreground detail and make out also across the bay, on the far shoreline, the chimney of the once very active Penzance Serpentine Works, the Queen's Hotel and St Peter's Church.

**Landing Fish,
Newlyn Old Harbour 1880s**

In sharp contrast to the previous photograph this image shows the high degree of activity once the fishing boats had landed with their catch. The *Eliza Jane* is seen here discharging her catch in the old harbour and Gibsons, the photographers, have done well to capture this very active scene with the relatively slow plates available at the time. There is some blurring of movement to be seen but this adds to the overall effect of intense activity.

Packing Fish, Newlyn c. 1890

Once the catch was landed the beaches and streets, processing sheds and backstreet cottage fish stores, became a hive of activity. This fine beach scene shows the baskets in which the fish were carried from the shore and children watching the menfolk at work. This, along with the images that follow, are the legacy left to us by the inspired efforts of early Cornish photographers. They help establish in us a strong sense of the vitality and tradition the fishing industry has always injected into the daily life of Newlyn, then and now.

Landing into the Old Newlyn Harbour, 1890s

Small craft are being used to convey fish from the larger boats a little further out in the bay, just out of sight beyond the old harbour wall. The fish merchants take their pick for selling on into the major markets, while jowsters are washing and preparing the fish, loading them directly into the waiting carts before they set off into the surrounding villages and hamlets where they will be offered sale.

Sorting the Fish c.1900

The fisher girl seen extreme right was Mary Wearne. She often modelled for several of the Newlyn School painters, Stanhope Forbes in particular. She is featured in two well known canvases, 'The Hopeless Dawn' and 'Last Rites'. Looking at this beautifully captured composition of fisherwomen sorting fish that they are about to carry into the town for sale, it is quite easy to see how the painters of the day were influenced from time to time by the photographers.

A Basket of Pilchards

Of unknown date, this photograph shows one of the typical backstreet yards with its fish cellar. Here a basket of pilchards has been brought in for processing and salting down.

Newlyn Fish Jowster

This woman on her selling round has stopped for the photographer at the top of Fore Street slip. The willow basket on her back, known as a 'cawal' or 'cowle', appears empty; one can only imagine how heavy it became at the beginning of her day laden with fish and salt. The broad band across her forehead took much of the weight, whilst a pad stuffed with horsehair was tied at waist level at the back, under the skirt, to further ease the burden during the miles walked. The workload hardly bears thinking about, and many similar photographs show in the carriage and demeanour of such women the harshness of their daily commitment to this way of life.

**Donkey Transport
Penzance c.1900**

The donkey was to be found everywhere as a willing, or as stories go, a most unwilling beast of burden. This photograph was taken in front of the row of cottages that make up Brighton Terrace which ran along the bottom of the later constructed Morrab Road in Penzance.

Trewarveneth Street, Newlyn c. 1900

This is typical of the cobbled streets which run quite steeply up the hill from the immediate old Newlyn harbour. Here the fish jowsters would have climbed with their heavy loads, calling at the cottage doors. The photograph conveys the variety of buildings in Newlyn, with its abundance of granite and cob cottages, fish cellars, boat- and basket-makers' sheds, along with some inviting inns. One such, no longer in existence, stood within a short distance of this scene – the 'Three Tuns'. The narrow inviting streets still survive here but the cobbled walkways have almost all disappeared; the last I saw being in Chapel Street.

Fish of the Day c.1890

The fish the old lady is holding appears to be a good-sized pollack. The photographer obviously thought it was worthwhile carrying his heavy plate camera and supporting gear down the slipway and into the old harbour to capture the event, though the donkey's face shows some resentment I feel at this interruption in the day's proceedings.

Jowster and Veteran, 1890s

This engaging street portrait is of John Divine, an old fish jowster. His real claim to fame was as a veteran hero of the Indian Mutiny (1857-58). A decoration he received during this campaign can be seen pinned to the left-hand side of his waistcoat.

Fishing Lugger on Penzance Promenade Beach, 1870s

Taken in the 1870s, the fishermen have hoisted the lugger's sails to dry whilst mending nets and 'brimming' ('breaming') the hull as one man can be seen doing. This process involved painting the vessel with a mixture of pitch and sulphur in order to preserve the hull. There was obviously a good breeze that day as the telling movement of the mizzen and mainsails show due to the extended exposure time necessary for the pre-1878 wet plates used. This introduces a pleasing visual feature into the composition, as well as providing a useful clue to dating the image, along with the local boat registration. Until 1869 Penzance boats were designated PE, but afterwards PZ preceded the numerals.

Newlyn Old Harbour, 1870s

This photograph was taken in the old Newlyn harbour around four hundred years after the first recorded request to the Bishop of Exeter, by one Edmond Lacy, for a contribution towards the establishment of a quay or jetty at Newlyn in the parish of Paul, dated 1435. An almost timeless atmosphere is projected to the viewer here, provoking thoughts on the slow pace of change in the centuries preceding this exposure being made, compared to the accelerating speed of changes since. As in the previous print, one man is 'brimming' the hull of a lugger, whilst the sails are hoisted for drying in a gentle breeze. Three young boys soak up the Victorian summer afternoon sun, quite unaware of the years that lie ahead for them.

Newlyn Cliff Road Conversation

The men here are all involved in the town's fishing, and are also all related. The Cotton family was typical of others in the town at the time, and such family ties were common throughout most of the fishing towns and coves in the county, as evidenced by the family gathering seen at Porthgwarra Cove later in this book.

Lower Newlyn, 1880s

I've included this general street scene of the area on which the Fish market was later to be built because it was rarely ever photographed, and as it shows a number of features that are open to interest. Fish sales were then held in the open air, most often on the beaches where the catch was landed, but also in the town in front of the area where the white merchants' huts are located in this photograph.

Street Fish Sale, early 1900s

The location of this sale of flat fish is shown in the previous photograph. The vigorous ringing of a hand bell was and still is the usual method of summoning merchants and others with an interest in the proceedings. Gone of course are sales in the streets, swept away by modern market regulations and the need to accommodate the larger size of catches.

St Peter's Fair, Newlyn, 1880s

Newlyn was once part of the parish of Paul and its fair was held in October during Paul Feast week. By the time this photograph was taken around the 1880s it was known as St Peter's Fair, named after the recently established Newlyn church. A contemporary description extracted from a book entitled *Down on the Western Sea* by an author identifying themselves as 'Old Cornish' conveys the event in a suitably Victorian graphic style, as follows. 'Then too the merry-go-rounds and swings and aunt Sallys and stalls for the sale of ginger bread and especially for fairins were established on that ridge of ground between the road and the river. There too, occupying the most commanding position might be seen Old Willy Shakespeare, the merry showman, a sort of King among the frivolous fraternity, so that by the time the evening had arrived, a lively and most excited crowd was assembled about the bank and the bridge'. The projection on the top of the roof, seen centre above the showmen's caravans, was the old pilot's lookout that disappeared following a fire which gutted the building in 1895.

St Peter's Fair Showman, 1880s

Whether his real name was Willy Shakespeare as mentioned in the previous caption supporting the St Peter's Fair print is open to question, there he is however, bowler-hatted up on the makeshift stage, looking fully in charge and not someone the children would want to upset. The water wheel seen top right is that of the once very busy Tolcarne Mill.

Plymouth Boats in Newlyn c.1880

Plymouth boats came mostly to Newlyn in the later part of the nineteenth century to pick up fish to transport it back for sale in that city. This fine photograph of a group of them in Newlyn old harbour was taken certainly before construction began on the north pier at the beginning of the 1890s, possibly late 1870s, or early 1880s.

Newlyn Harbour, 1890s

Looking south-west across the harbour, the north arm was still to have widening work done and other constructions added.

Afternoon Sun-break

Surely one of the Newlyn School artists is hovering just out of the view to quickly sketch this Newlyn cottage door scene for his next painting.

LT303 *Chamois*

Lowestoft fishing boats used Newlyn for a long time, stretching well into the twentieth century, as a base port throughout the seasons. Here the *Chamois* has, with an amazing demonstration of late nineteenth century inspired photographic technique, been captured as she makes a final dash in the south-easterly gale, running before the wind for Newlyn harbour. The camera could only have been positioned on the south pier to obtain this wonderfully stirring image and, ironically, moves to improve Newlyn as a safe haven, the first by the building of this pier completed in 1886, had been both sadly but dramatically promoted by the effect on the authorities of the loss with all hands of the 14-ton Newlyn lugger *Jane* on 7 October 1880. Having only Penzance harbour to seek refuge in, and running across the following sea in close sight of safety she slid into the trough of the heavy breakers, was rolled over and sank immediately, drowning all seven men on board.

St Ives – the Railway Approach

Draycott Hill provided the vantage point for the photographer Daphne Pearson to achieve this wonderfully detailed view of the railway approach to St Ives. The growing numbers of tourists arriving in the late nineteenth and early twentieth century on this GWR branchline from St Erth, would have been treated to an intoxicating cocktail of seaside smells, a mixture of locomotive steam and fresh Atlantic sea air wafting across Porthminster beach, the final ingredient being a heady mix of tar and drying pilchard nets as they passed the many seine boats laid up on both sides of the approach viaduct. After the middle of the 1920s this view would have changed; the companies that ran the seine fishing ventures had all disappeared and the boats broken up.

St Ives Harbour

This is the view of St Ives that never fails to stir the senses as one approaches the town from Tregenna Hill. Fishing boats are shown about to leave on the high tide but the number of these seen here gives no idea of the four hundred or so that once made up one of the largest fleets in Europe in the mid-nineteenth century. As the fleet make it out into the bay they will pass the extended Smeaton's Pier.

Smeaton's Pier

Named after its engineer, Smeaton's Pier is on the north side of St Ives harbour beach. The foundation stone was laid down in June 1888 and it was eventually finished in 1910 after an extension was added to the earlier work. This print was made from one half of a stereo card pair.

Smeaton's Pier from the North End c.1900

From the outset this pier has always been the centre of great activity. In the early 1900s when this photograph was made, fishing boats and coastal sailing craft such as the barque seen here would fill the harbour so that it was possible to walk from one vessel to the next across the entire span of the harbour to the west pier, the beginnings of which had been established in 1894. Today the relatively small numbers of fishing boats are joined by numerous pleasure craft of various shapes and sizes which have brought a different life and interest to animate the scene.

A St Ives' Mackerel Boat c.1890

This is a fine example of the type of boat used by the St Ives mackerel fleet throughout the nineteenth and early twentieth century. They would sail to fishing grounds often twenty to thirty miles west of St Ives, drift netting. This would apply only in the winter and spring seasons as the warmer sea temperatures of summer and autumn encouraged the mackerel to move closer to the land when the smaller boats of the inshore fishermen were employed on catching them using hand-lines. Pilchards in great shoals would also come in and these larger boats would then concentrate their efforts more on catching these. A saying used throughout the fishing communities in Cornwall: 'When the corn is in the shock, then the fish are on the rock'.

Skinning a Dogfish, early 1900s

The harbour beach, always another location for a variety of activities, presents a view here of dogfish being skinned on the shingle just in front of the Sloop Inn. Nothing was wasted and the man on the left is seen loading skins into his cart, the rough skin, known as shagreen, being used as a sandpaper in furniture making. Dogfish is still sold as 'rock salmon' in fish and chip shops

Porthminster Beach c.1900

In contrast to the previous print is this view of the Monet-like impressionist picture of Porthminster beach. From the late 1890s onwards the newly emerging tourist had begun to arrive in ever-growing numbers on the GWR steam trains at the little branchline station overlooking this beach, as shown in the photograph earlier in the section.

An Ice Cream Vendor, St Ives c.1900

Easterbrooks of Hayle and St Ives with their celebrated ice creams made in premises at the top of Longstone Hill, Carbis Bay, were on hand to supply the growing number of tourists. Announced 'absolutely pure' on the canopy of this elegant little cart, one presumes this notice applies to the ice cream rather than to the young salesman as he gazes soulfully into the camera for this delightful turn-of-the-nineteenth century photograph by Humphreys of St Ives.

Tregenna Place and High Street, 1890s

The lower stretch of this main road into St Ives from Carbis Bay was at one time called Green Court. It is now known as Tregenna Place and leads down from Tregenna Hill and round to High Street at the end of which we come to the Parish Church of St Ives (St Ia's). After this we move into old St Ives with its fascinating maze of back streets, courtyards, alleys, hidden gardens and squares, cobbled walkways, all forming a huddle against the worst excesses of the North Atlantic gales in winter, while providing secluded locations to mend nets, salt down pilchards, repair canvas, etc., shaded from the heat and brilliant light of a summer's day. By the later half of the nineteenth century, artists along with the photographers were appearing in ever-increasing numbers, as in Newlyn, to soak up the colour and vitality of St Ives. Though the traditional way of life was interrupted by the activity of these incomers, we have also to thank them for the legacy of images they have left us. The short selection of photographs which follow will help to give some hint of the old town's character, still fortunately viewable today, once one gets away from some of the brassy excesses inflicted on certain frontages alongside the harbour beach.

Virgin Street, St Ives

There is something rather fishy about this image taken from an old postcard. The publisher looks to have been intent on amplifying the idea that has been put forward over the years, that St Ives can sport some of the country's biggest cats, and more of them than any other town or village in the county, due to the plentiful supply of fish leftovers available to feed them on. However five cats all the same size and tone, surrounded in three cases by a tell-tale lightened area needs questioning! Otherwise its certainly true about the cats of St Ives; I've seen some whoppers during my own wanderings around the back streets.

Back Road and Porthmeor Square, St Ives, 1890s

Both these photographs have been made from early celluloid film negatives which I discovered over thirty years ago in a tattered envelope sandwiched between some dusty glass plates. The negative base-material was a clue to the fact that they had been exposed in one of the first roll film cameras introduced by Kodak at the end of the nineteenth century. It was however with both surprise and pleasure that on viewing I saw they depicted St Ives, since the rest of the glass negatives were of unknown family groups. Enlarging them has of course amplified the grain in the image gained from this early roll film, but marvellously added atmosphere and a canvas-like texture, recalling the subject matter and painting style of the artists working in the studios nearby. The image of the hurrying women who so perfectly animate the Porthmeor Square print signals the possibilities that were opened up to the amateur photographer by Kodak's introduction of the snapshot camera. It is less likely that professionals with their heavy plate gear would have attempted this random grab-shot exposure.

Chapel Court, St Ives, early 1900s

Taken in the early 1900s this photograph offers an inviting glimpse of one of the sheltered back street areas in Downalong St Ives, referred to previously. This, fortunately, is a feature still to be found, St Ives having escaped the worst excesses of developers who have disfigured so many fishing villages and towns in Cornwall.

Mending Crayfish and Crab Nets

This relaxed view of net mending taking place on Smeaton's Pier St Ives, provides an appropriate end to this glimpse into the life of the two fishing towns. It shows an activity that would have been carried on in the small coastal towns and coves throughout Cornwall in the nineteenth and first half of the twentieth centuries.

THE LAND'S END PENINSULA

Rowe's Farm, Penzance 1891

Urban Penzance very quickly gave way to the countryside in the nineteenth century as the first two photographs in this section show. Taken on the promenade, to the south-west of the built-up area, the fields of Rowe's farm, like many others then, reached to the very edge of the back gardens and doorsteps of the town dwellers. The farmhouse is here seen on the right of the picture with the surrounding fields covered in the snow of March 1891, the year of the Great Blizzard. Alexandra Road had been ceremonially opened in 1865 by the Princess of Wales herself, when the splendid centrepiece lamp had been erected also, to dedicate and mark the occasion.

Hosking's Alexandra Dairy
c.1890

Named by Mr Hoskings the dairy farmer sometime after Princess Alexandra's visit to Penzance in 1865, the farmhouse is of an earlier date as can be seen. It survived well into the twentieth century and a friend of mine can remember being sent there with a jug and basket as a small girl, when on holiday visits to her aunt in Penzance, from Pendeen, to collect cream and eggs. Now children of all ages sail boats on the pool constructed where it once stood, whilst swans have replaced the chickens.

Wherrytown Beach, 1870s

A short distance across the road from Hoskings Dairy, shown in the previous print, was the Wherrytown Promenade beach providing a haven in fine weather for the fishermen to lay up their boats and tend their gear. Here also stood bathing machines, used by Victorian ladies to reach a submerged state in the briny without the threat of body exposure of any kind. This was further promoted by beach regulations that made it necessary for men and women to take the waters at separate times in the day. The photograph was made in the 1870s, sometime before the building which is seen directly above the men's changing hut, known as 'Mr Norton's Royal Promenade Baths', was demolished in 1883.

Excursions c.1900

With the boom in tourism of the late nineteenth and early twentieth century, the Jersey-cart tour into the remoter parts of West Penwith became a must to complete the holiday. Penzance Promenade was full of local operators of this form of transport. Rowe's Farm, shown previously standing in fields to the right of Alexandra Road, has completely vanished under the weight of development. The print above was made just over a decade after the photograph of Rowe's farm. Much of this new building catered for the growth in visitors and comprised small family hotels and guesthouses.

Newlyn Combe and the River, 1870s

This photograph of the Tolcarne area of Newlyn was taken in the 1870s, well before the dawn of tourist excursions. The old bridge seen here was the only entry into lower Newlyn town from Penzance, and to reach Mousehole a climb up the steep hill out and around through Paul village was necessary. By the late 1890s however, a second bridge had been added and the road that linked Newlyn directly with Mousehole, following the shoreline, had been completed.

Mousehole, early 1900s

The village and harbour are viewed here from the end of the western arm of the quayside, showing the main road coming into the village from Newlyn just to the right. Fish nets are hung to dry on the harbour rails after 'barking', a process applied to preserve and protect them.

Mousehole and Harbour c.1930

This photograph gives a good view of the cluster of harbourside cottages in Mousehole in the first half of the twentieth century. It would appear to be a scene from the 1930s judging by the children's dress. Also, in my enlargement, I can just make out the shape of a bus (centre right of the Ship Inn) which appears to be of that period.

Old Pilot's Lookout, Mousehole c.1900

This description appears on the back of the original print I have and could possibly have been used for this purpose before being used as living accommodation, as it obviously was by the time this photograph was made in the early 1900s. It does provide a telling picture of the wonderfully textured make up of these Mousehole backstreet cottages and walkways.

Dolly Pentreath's Cottage, Mousehole, 1890s

The wealth of detail and architectural pattern seen in this photograph of another backstreet Mousehole cottage further illustrates what I remarked on in the previous print. Dolly Pentreath, an old fisherwoman who once lived here, was said to be the last person to have spoken the Cornish language naturally and fluently. This has been questioned by some who have suggested that she simply gabbled nonsense to visitors and strangers for small gifts of money. Dr Borlase of Castle Horneck however, a respected local magistrate, showed he had no doubts about her claim by stating in 1774 that she spoke Cornish as readily as others did English. Six years prior to that a scholar, Daines Barrington, making a tour of the county in 1768 to find out about the ancient language, said he had tracked down only one old Mousehole women, Dolly Pentreath, who spoke it fluently to several aged neighbours who also understood much that she said.

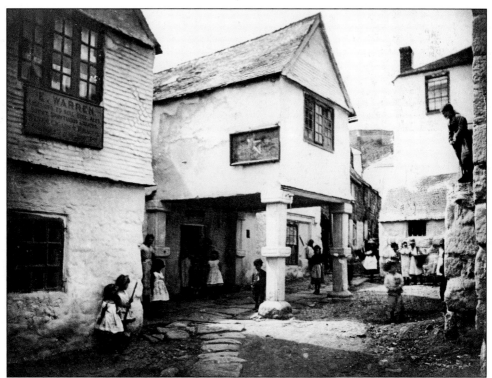

The Keigwin Arms, Mousehole

This fifteenth-century building survived the onslaught of Spanish invaders who, on 23 July in 1595, landed in Mousehole and burnt down most of the village, before going on to wreak havoc in other parts of the immediate locality. Richard Carew's *Survey of Cornwall* of 1602 gives a detailed account of the brief but vicious and damaging attack on the village when Jenkin Keigwin, the master of the house, was killed as he attempted to defend the village against the overwhelming two-hundred-strong Spanish force. Seen here (one of a number of photographs I have of the building) when it was an inn, it still survives as one of the only complete examples of an early manor house in West Penwith.

Newbridge and Trembath Mill c.1880

An excursion to Land's End from Penzance would have taken the road passing through Newbridge, seen here, now on the main A30. Water from the fast-flowing river was diverted to form this pool which then supplied the leat-whose waters powered the large wheels of Trembath Mill, a quarter of a mile distant across the fields lower down.

Trembath Mill

This watermill and the Tolcarne Mill at Newlyn were two of the most important in the area and both were equipped with two working wheels. The largest of the two, at Trembath, was 25 feet in diameter, bigger than any other in West Penwith.

Bossava Mill, Lamorna, 1860s

The coastal road from Mousehole brings you eventually down into Lamorna and to Bossava Mill. This exterior view of it appears of quite early photographic technique common to prints from the 1860s, which is when I think it was made. If so its the earliest photograph I have of a Penwith Mill and is typical of the many that were once dotted along the length of valley streams all over Cornwall in the nineteenth century, and for a number of centuries before.

Bossava Mill Interior

This is a rare interior photograph in which flashlight powder has been used for illumination. From information given to me in the past by Kenneth Major B.Arch, RIBA, FSA, an enthusiast and authority on mills, I am able to cast some further light on the subject.

The granite millstones are contained in a circular tun, grain from sacks being fed slowly into the hopper at the top prior to grinding. A windlass mounted on posts (seen top right), hoisted up sacks of grain as they were brought in. At the head of the steps the large wingnut was the means by which the runner stone was raised or lowered, as it acted on the horizontal bar just viewable reaching underneath the tun. The large pit wheel is the first gear wheel on the main shaft, whilst a lantern gear located on the stone spindle behind the chute was engaged by the waterwheel on the far-side wall. The chute can be seen clearly pointing towards the two shaking sieves into which it would have discharged the newly-ground flour.

The heightened noise level from all this activity has to be experienced to be fully appreciated, as I once did, during a grinding session many years ago at Clapper Mill located at the top of the valley in Lamorna. William Clemens was both the farmer and miller and operated it then to grind up corn and maize for cattle feed. Dust from the grain husks added a further fascination to the experience, raising a cocktail of earthy smells, whilst the whole building seemed to throb with a life all its own, as if the opening of the sluice allowing the water to drive the wheel had charged up hidden arteries in every corner.

Flower Pickers – Early Twentieth Century

The sheltered valleys and lightly wooded hillsides of the south-west side of the Land's End peninsula offered ideal conditions for the cultivation of daffodils and violets. Mousehole, Lamorna, coastal smallholdings in St Buryan and St Levan, would all see early January flowers ready to be gathered and sent away to the major cities by rail.

Flower picking above Mousehole

A camera break in the afternoon's proceedings.

Trewoofe Manor House, Lamorna c.1890

A walking excursion continuing on from Lamorna in the late nineteenth century, when this photograph was made, could well take you past this fine example of a medieval doorway, a remaining feature of the once important Trewoofe manor house, the seat of the de Trewoofe family (pronounced Trove), first mentioned in records of 1270. The house is located at the head of the Lamorna valley, but during the last century the heavy granite entrance surround made the journey completely across the peninsula to St Ives and back again under the direction of the present owner, Margaret Powell. Having taken on ownership in the 1970s of the once grand house, but now minus a number of its former architectural features, including this original porch bearing the family arms, which had been removed some sixty years earlier, Margaret was determined on restoring the house to something of its former glory. On discovering the portal was still in existence, she worked to have it returned. With great resolve this she has done, and her absorbing account of this and Trewoofe's history is given in her booklet *The Story of a Cornish House*. A public footpath passes close by, but the splendid old butter churn seen in the photograph has yet to be rediscovered.

Boskenna, St Buryan, 1909

Cornwall was well endowed with rural manor houses, particularly in those valley locations traversing the more sheltered length of the south coast, though Boskenna Manor in St Buryan Parish, approximately two miles further south-west from Lamorna, stands fairly exposed to the gales that sweep in from Biscay and the Atlantic.

The twenty-two staff seen here would have been a typical complement at the time of similar households

throughout the county. The little girl Elizabeth (Miss Betty) Paynter aged two, sitting with her father and mother, Colonel and Mrs Paynter, asked me to copy this photograph and if possible to improve on the fading original print in her possession in the 1970s. A book by Jim Hosking *People, Places and Past Events in St Buryan* gives an extended account of life and times at Boskenna in the first half of the twentieth century.

Thatched Round Houses

In the nineteenth century it was still possible to find simple cottage dwellings still inhabited, the style of which date back into prehistory. A number were of a round or semi-round construction, and it is fortunate that they had survived long enough for the introduction of photography to provide us with a visual record of them. Four examples are shown here.

Grumbla Round House, Parish of Sancreed

Boleigh Cottage

Having climbed the hill out of Lamorna this dwelling was located at Boleigh, in St Buryan Parish. The last battle between the Cornish and the English is recorded as having taken place on this site in the year AD935.

Crous-an-Wra, House and Shop

Situated on the road to Land's End, north-west of St Buryan village was William Warren's house and shop – licensed to sell snuff and tobacco the noticeboard tells us. The place-name today is subject to a variety of spellings, often written Croes-an-Wray, and is said to mean, in Cornish, 'the witches cross'.

Chapel Idne, Sennen

This already ancient dwelling on the cliffpath into Sennen Cove, one mile from Land's End, was built on the site of an even earlier holy house dating from the eleventh century from which it took its name, no doubt utilizing much of the original stonework.

William Trewerne's Farm, St Levan Parish c.1908

Charles Roberts Chapple, a gifted amateur photographer, was on hand on a summer's day around 1908 to capture this wonderfully evocative scene. Everyone rests for a moment during what looks to be the harvesting of a crop of oats using a horse-drawn binder. William Trewern, wearing the sun hat, looks on obviously pleased with the way things have progressed.

Harvest Dinner, Trewey Farm

A sit-down midday dinner was a much enjoyed ritual and a looked-for occasion at all the main harvest times. This photograph was also made by Charles Chapple, and quite probably on the same day as previous exposures he had made, one of which precedes this. William Trewern sits at the head of the table as one would expect. The exposure has been achieved using only the available light from the window of the farmhouse and says much for the photographer's skill with the fairly simple quarter-plate camera I know he used.

Fishermen of Porthgwarra Cove, 1880s

Situated just a few miles to the south of Land's End, Porthgwarra was in the 1880s, about the time this photograph was made, a small but thriving fishing community. Three families, the Rowe's, Harvey's and Jacksons provided most of the fishermen in the community and were joined by the Rawling's living nearby in a cottage on the cliffpath to St Levan. Crayfish netting, lobster and crab pot laying, hand-lining and some seine net fishing were all carried on in what can only be described as demanding conditions in the turbulent currents around this end of the peninsula.

Interior of a Cornish Cottage

Described as the living room of Billy Harvey's cottage at Porthgwarra by one author, I have reservations about this, since conflicting claims have been made as to its possible location. My own original print has handwritten on the back 'Cornish Kitchen', and it's most certainly representative of many that were once to be found throughout the county. Wonderfully detailed and full of homely interest, the alarm clock on the dresser gives the time of day as 12.32, whilst the hanging wall clock shows 12.44, so we know the photographer had used the available midday window light to make the exposure. The prints and photographs in the room display no reference to the sea or fishing which I feel would be the case if indeed it was of a fisherman's cottage. However it offers a fascinating glimpse into an aspect of the past rarely seen, and sits well alongside the previous picture of the cove.

The First and Last Post Office in England c.1900

Pausing to post a letter or card carrying the special postmark offered by Sennen Post Office was a must for many visitors making the final last mile to Land's End, when this photograph was made in the first years of the 1900s.

A steep hillside road separates Sennen Village from Sennen Cove, perhaps one should add *very* steep to this directive, since in the past it seems the communities were separated into fishermen down below, and farmers and other craftsmen up top, and who would want to climb that hill out of the cove very often anyway? I did it the other day and decided that it was rather late in life to take up mountaineering! This shows one of the seine companies' pilchard boats being unloaded on the main beach, prior to carting the fish to the processing shed in the cove for salting and pressing down into barrels. The pilchard fishing was always worked by a company since the costs involved in setting up with a seine net, good size seine boat, tuck boat and other necessary gear, required a financial investment beyond that of one man or even a fishing family.

**Land's End Hotel –
GWR Bus no.39 c.1910**

The hotel at this most westerly tip of the country has seen a multitude of comings and goings. The Great Western Railway couldn't manage to get a railway line to reach it so they did the next best thing, as seen here.

London to Land's End and Back

The Easter week-end saw this valiant group pitting their wits against the formidable road miles and conditions between this remote Cornish headland and the capital city. Today, but for the fact that by easter all Cornish trunk roads are being dug up or otherwise arranged to frustrate rapid progress into and out of the county, visiting motorists would be denied the same challenge and sense of achievement they still enjoy, as did these early enthusiasts and knights of the road, on finally reaching their destination.

Land's End from the Air, 1937

Taken with an aircraft camera, this is as Land's End looked from above on 16 July 1937.

Opposite page, bottom: **Land's End Airfield**

The small airfield situated between Land's End and St Just-in-Penwith became operational in the latter half of the 1930s. Nearly always busy today, it continues to offer a service to Scilly and scenic flights, as it did from the beginning when this first aircraft, a seven-seater de Havilland Dragon, was purchased from Irish Sea Airways. Here she is seen with the staff of Channel Air Ferries Ltd, who ran things then, photographed on the airfield with Chapel Carn Brea hill in the background. A very sad end was to befall this aircraft, its passengers and pilot, when on 3 June 1941, whilst on a flight to the Scilly Isles, it was shot down by a hostile German war plane, most likely a Condor. The only explanation put forward over the years for the execution of such a brutal act against what was clearly a small unarmed passenger plane, is that in a patch of poor visibility over the sea the Dragon may have been mistaken for a military aircraft, though this has never been established.

RAF Float Planes over St Mary's, Scilly

This aerial photograph of two Saro London floatplanes from 204 Squadron of the RAF was made by another of these aircraft, flying in formation on the same day as the previous exposure over Land's End was made, 16 July 1937. The original negatives and prints conveyed the date, time and other relevant details printed for official records along their edges. Those involved here were from the group of five from this squadron who in the second half of that year cruised to New South Wales. All had long range fuel tanks fitted and these can be clearly seen fixed to the fuselage, directly under the top wing.

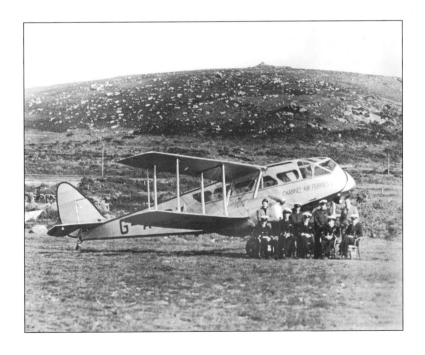

St Just-in-Penwith

Arriving at Penzance on the Great Western Railway in the nineteenth century many visitors could be excused for thinking that they had arrived at the very last town in the far west of the country. An array of horse transport would have been the only means of embarking on exploration into the hinterland. Imagine then their surprise on being informed that ten miles further west, perched almost on the edge of the cliffs facing three thousand miles of the Atlantic, was a mining town, St Just-in-Penwith. Certainly the contrast established by the rest of the peninsula's reliance on farming and fishing as the dominant sources of employment, set the tin mining community of St Just apart, promoting in a number of interesting ways individual characteristics to both the place and its people. The two inter-connected squares are in themselves a feature not found elsewhere, almost more French in style than English. Three photographs that follow were taken in these squares.

Market Square, St Just-in-Penwith

The scene features St Just parish church, the GWR service bus, and Archelaus's horse bus, which also had the license to carry the Royal Mail up to the end of the year 1920.

Scene in Bank Square, St Just-in-Penwith

Mr Harvey operated the Queen Street Bakery.

Wellington Hotel, St Just-in-Penwith

Ben Eddy's horse bus, the Loyal, was operated by the landlord of the Wellington Hotel.

Tin Miners, St Just-in-Penwith

This is an early photograph of miners taken by Edwin Trembath who had established a studio in the town in 1860. The man centre top, without a helmet, was Captain Henry Boyns who was in charge of the underground arrangements when the Prince of Wales and Princess Alexandra visited the Crowns group of mines at Botallack in St Just on Monday 24 July 1865, and descended the Boscawen diagonal shaft.

Princess Alexandra, 24 July 1865

After surfacing from the depths of the mine at Botallack, the Princess was photographed holding the small pick hammer with which she had ceremoniously used to chip away a souvenir piece of tin during her tour underground. A photograph in my previous book, *Lost Cornwall* presents a picture of the beginning of the Royal couple's descent into the mine, and viewing the terrain, even on the cliff surface, gives some idea why the Princess felt unsteady and rather shaken on completing what she had found to be quite an ordeal. She was driven fairly quickly afterwards to St Michael's Mount to recuperate.

Top: **Wheal Geevor**

The nineteenth century saw the horse whim still much in use for hauling ore in kibbles (massive iron buckets) to the surface. The horse was walked around harnessed to the vertical shaft attached to the large cross beam. Wheal Geevor at Pendeen, near St Just, was the last mine in the area to close as a fully working tin mine, but still operates as a tourist attraction, with museum displays and organised underground visits.

Above: **Ingots of Tin**

Ingots ready for collection. I've not been able to establish for certain where this photograph was taken. The barrels in the picture would possibly be holding salted-down pilchards, ready for export by sea, so Penzance or Hayle Dock would be likely locations. It is however a sight that would once have been common around Cornwall in and near to major mining areas.

The Old Levant Mine, Pendeen

Situated near to Pendeen, a short journey from St Just on the north coast road, the old Levant mine is shown here during its working life. It can still be seen today in its restored condition, promoted by the Trevithick Society, though it hasn't worked since 1919. Once celebrated for the amount of tin and copper it produced, it was the scene that year of one of the worst mining disasters in Cornwall when the man-engine (which conveyed men up and down to the various working levels) suddenly collapsed during a change of shifts, killing 31 miners.

Zennor, 1890s

Continuing along the north coast road past the hamlet of Morvah brings you eventually to Zennor, the last village before reaching St Ives. Church and chapel are seen, but the thatched roof near to the church is all that's visible of the Tinners Arms in this late nineteenth century photograph. The houses huddle close, affording some protection against the worst excesses of the north Atlantic winter weather, for there is an almost complete absence of trees. Today the huge granite boulders are less obvious as bushes, trees and other vegetation have grown along the boundary walls and small gardens, softening the approach from the hill, especially in spring and summer.

Eglosmeor Mill, Zennor

This little water mill once stood on the path that still leads out past the church towards the Zennor cliffs. On 12 November 1894 a flood swept down the valley from the hills above Foage, taking Eglosmeor Mill with it on it's destructive progress towards the sea. James Cousins and Thomas Perry were the working millers at the time, having not long taken over the holding from James Stevens and his family who had worked it for some thirty years prior.

Zennor Church Interior

This nineteenth-century interior view of Zennor church shows features dating well back to the seventeenth century. The 'Horse Box' pews, for those families not wishing to mingle with the lower orders, and the wooden gallery at the end where at one time local musicians would have played for the service, were swept away by the Victorians' zeal for restoration, along with the homely plasterwork.

Zennor Mermaid

This medieval bench-end in Zennor Church with its carved figure of a mermaid, is surrounded by mystery and, it is said, remains to warn young men of the village to beware of the fatal charms of a local mermaid. Legend has it that in ancient times, a young sailor disappeared, never to be seen again, after having been entranced by her singing drifting up from the sea over the headland. Lured down to the cove by her siren call, and thence further into the sea to meet her, she held him in her drowning embrace, swimming far out in to the blue green depths. A strange local occurrence is associated with a walk along the cliffs in a light sea mist, and to be suddenly startled on hearing the eerie cries of seals from the small island off St Ives. The rocky hollows, dark inlets in the steep cliffs and caves, further increase the effect of their echoing their cries. I experienced this phenomenon on several occasions myself during the five years I lived in Zennor Parish, sometimes being chillingly amazed when the sound was amplified from a seal that had obviously swum close inshore. Is this the Mermaid of our legend?

Tremedda Cottage, 1914

Tremedda is just a few short cliff fields north of Zennor village, renowned for its swift weather changes, often from one type of fog to another. I find something quite haunting about this scene taken as the sea mist encloses the small party of people waiting one morning in 1914 for the bride, Miss Annie Osborne, to emerge from her cottage home to be driven in style to Zennor Church, there to wed the young Jim Berryman. Florence Dow of Talland House, St Ives, had sent the carriage with her coachman as a wedding gesture, the bride's family being tenants of her daughter, Elsie, who owned all of Tremedda Farm and its tied cottages. Happily, unlike the fate of the sailor mesmerized by the Zennor mermaid of misty legend, young Jim was to find happiness with the girl of his choice that day, taking her to live in Towednack village nearby.

Country Wedding, 28 October 1939

This single, simple, delightfully unpretentious wedding photograph with everyone happily posed together in front of a fine crop of cabbages and cauliflowers in the kitchen garden, seems to impart so much fun and visually radiated warmth to the record of the occasion, that the over-mannered extensive and expensive album concoctions many present-day aficionados completely fail to achieve. Miss Lorraine Bottrell had just married Mr Tredinnick in nearby Ludgvan Church and although the late contrasty autumn sunlight may have given Mr Richards, the photographer, a few problems getting the exposure, everyone seems to be enjoying the day and smiling at the right moment. The photo-call in no way lasted longer than was necessary to change the plate holder round for a second go at things, so that guests could soon reach the excellent spread waiting inside Sunny Corner cottage here at Cockwells. Hat styles are back in fashion as I write, well almost!.

Madron Workhouse, early 1900s

Another road running south, inland from the north coast at Morvah towards Penzance, takes you through Madron village where this workhouse once stood. Much is known and has already been written about these infamous institutions that were once sited throughout the whole country. Certainly this forbidding edifice presents the viewer with the grimmest of thoughts and did so in the past I'm told by those who remember their grandparents' fears about such places. Built in 1838 to serve the prescribed needs of around 400 people throughout West Cornwall , its final role was that of an old person's hospital. The St Ives primitive artist Alfred Wallis ended his days here in 1942, just nine years before it was closed in 1951.

Kenegie Farm, early 1900s

An injection of fresh air is provided here in contrast to the vision of Madron workhouse life. This early autumn scene was taken in the first half of the 1900s in Gulval, the parish adjacent to Madron, during a break in cutting and carting the first of the cauliflower crop on Kenegie Manor home farm.

Opposite: **Polly's Cottage**

'Polly's Cottage, Gulval', was written on the back of this wonderfully animated scene dating from the 1880s, just that. I'm unable to cast any further light on the subject or discover whether Polly had more than the seven children already present, but it's a favourite photograph of mine and one I always enjoy looking at.

Threshing, West Cornwall c.1900

This print of September threshing is from a number of similar photographs in my collection. Most have probably been taken by the family amateur, usually with a simple camera at an informal photo call, followed by a snapshot approach. It's this which nearly always adds to the naturalness of the compositions and the feeling of nostalgia evoked on viewing these sun-drenched time capsules from the fields of a century ago.

**Marazion Baker
early 1900s**

This early 1900s view of Mr Truscott the Baker and his family in Marazion main street seemed an obvious follow-on to the threshing scene just featured. 'School Teas and Pic-Nic Parties catered for', reads the sign above the door.

Gulval Meet, early 1900s

The Western Hunt meet outside the Gulval Inn and church, and almost everything in the vicinity has now turned up except the fox, who's totally unaware at this point that he's inspired this grand and hugely popular get together.

Hillside Above Mount's Bay

Just east of Marazion, this field labourer is working on the site of an ancient open-cast copper mine, near Perranuthnoe village. The traditional Cornish shovel he's using to turn the ground is an excellent tool, and much-used throughout the county, particularly on hill-sides and heavy soils, the long hilt giving extra leverage when braced across the upper knee.

North Road, Goldsithney c.1900

Goldsithney is also just a little further east of Marazion, and this very engaging street scene was made around the turn of the last century.

Prussia Cove 1880 – Smuggler's Cottage

Prussia cove is linked with centuries of smuggling and there are a number of accounts written which deal at length with this. Certainly in the weather conditions smugglers would most likely have chosen to conceal their activities, early and late hours of the day, in morning mists and disturbed sea conditions, or in the deep shrouding colours of a late summer's evening, a strong, forbidding atmosphere pervades. The sheer cliffs and unrelenting grey of the rocky shore further amplify this chilling experience.

Foundry Square, Hayle, early 1900s

In 1779 John Harvey, a blacksmith from the village of Carnell Green, decided to establish workshops in Hayle town for the making of cast iron pumps. Having successfully set this up, he went on to add trading in a number of other commodities to the venture, including coal and timber. Henry, his son, further extended the scope of the company's business by introducing tin smelting and shipbuilding. As I have already said in my previous publication of photographs *Lost Cornwall*, the name Harveys of Hayle became known throughout the world at the height of their activities in the nineteenth century, and always predominates in published histories where the town's contribution to the Industrial

Revolution is mentioned. By the time this photograph was taken, however, the demise of mining and many of the associated industries meant the foundry was no longer viable; it closed in 1903.

Copperhouse, Hayle, early 1900s

The Cornish Copper Company of John Edwards also played a leading part in the business life of Hayle during the late eighteenth century and first half of the nineteenth century. For some years he established rival ventures to those of Harveys, and Copperhouse gets its name from the foundry with its copper smelter he set up at this other end of the town. A recession that hit the area towards the middle of the century badly affected this company and it failed, forcing its closure in 1840. When this photograph was made J F Pool metal perforators, had a factory on what had been part of the Copper Company site, behind the shops on the left. The dome of the old Market House, now removed, is just visible centrally above the people and the horse and carts.

The SS *Hayle*

Built by Harveys, the 300 ton steam ship *Hayle* was first launched in 1893 and is seen here in her home dock. Used mostly as a coal boat it was decided after a short while to provide her with more carrying capacity. Sent to Southampton to have the work done, they cut the whole vessel in half and added twenty feet in the middle to lengthen her hold. It is said that this made her somewhat difficult to manoeuvre in certain sea conditions, such as those for instance found on the estuary approach to the town dock, and this was probably the cause of her running aground several times on Hayle Bar. She was sold in 1921 to a firm in Liverpool.

Pannier Tank Locomotive 9717

At one time it would have been an everyday sight to see busy locomotives trundling about Hayle dock area, pulling trucks, steaming along beside the road quay to service the shipping, or crossing to the power station that once dominated the skyline. This 5700 class pannier tank steam locomotive has been halted on the track which ran directly to the power station and represents the only record I have come across taken in this location featuring the railway and local staff. I've included it for that reason and because it has aroused much interested comment already when shown around, particularly from enthusiasts of Cornish steam train history.

Penzance to Helston Horse Bus c.1890

This is the Penzance, Helston, Penryn to Falmouth Express horse bus, passing the bottom of Britains Hill as it leaves Penzance on its twenty-two mile journey to Falmouth. It' dates from around the late 1880s or early 1890s as far as I can establish, and, although the railways were well established in the county by then, much of the day-to-day travel between the main towns was still carried out using horse-drawn transport. The horses would most probably have been changed for a new team at Helston, and then harnessed up again later on the the return through to Penzance.

FALMOUTH

In recent years several quite comprehensive books have appeared documenting nineteenth and twentieth century Falmouth. So with this in mind, and knowing that my fairly small collection showing general views of the town would add little to what has already been published, I decided to the present the following snapshot glimpse contained in the family album of one of the town's most prominent artists of the day. I have recently been able to add a selection from this important album to my own collection due to the interest and kind support of Margaret Powell of Lamorna.

Charles Napier Hemy RA, RWS 1841–1917   Henry Scott Tuke, RA, RWS. 1858–1929

FALMOUTH FAMILY ALBUM OF CHARLES NAPIER HEMY R.A. R.W.S.

Charles Napier Hemy RA, RWS 1841–1917, and Henry Scott Tuke RA, RWS 1858–1929 were two of the foremost artists in Falmouth during the later half of the nineteenth century and first years of the twentieth century. Both had a great interest in marine painting and, following Hemy's example, Tuke was also to acquire a boat on which to paint, converting it likewise into a painting studio. Of the two men it was Hemy who concentrated almost exclusively on sea scenes, influenced by his first-hand working experience gathered as a ship's crewman in his early life. The vibrant, billowing, often heroic sailing ship paintings he achieved were much sought after during his lifetime by admirers and collectors, and he was to become wealthy. Because of this he was able to support the large family he and his second wife brought up in the house, known as Churchfields, he had specially built near to the Catholic church in Falmouth. His grand-daughter Margaret Powell is the author of a recent book about his life and work titled *Master of the Sea,* and she invited me to look through her grandparents snapshot albums and to make any copy negatives I wanted. Much of the photography, taken by various members of the family, reflects Hemy's great interest with the sea life of the town, showing also that it played an important part in their social lives. Henry Tuke was a friend of the family and the portrait of him and the print of his studio interior were amongst the collection.

Regatta-Day Outing

One is easily reminded of the subject matter chosen by post-impressionist painters in this and several other of the photographs that follow.

Above and opposite page, top: **Ladies' Day, Falmouth Sailing Club, c.1902–3**

Penryn Regatta Day

BEACH PHOTOGRAPHY – NAPIER HEMY'S FAMILY

Taking a snapshot of the snap-shot photographer.

Hilda and Barbara 1906.

The *Barbara*

Henry Tuke, like Napier Hemy, was very keen on being involved with the local maritime activities, as well as painting it. Here at Penryn regatta his yacht *Barbara* is seen on the right.

CHARLES NAPIER HEMY'S STUDIOS

The *Vanderveld,* Floating Studio

The first of these two photographs is of the *Vanderveld* which Napier Hemy, seen here on board, converted and used as a studio. It served him well for six years, providing a sympathetic environment in which he painted some of his best early marine pictures, but in 1897 it was suddenly wrecked whilst moored up a creek in bad weather.

The *Vandermeer* Floating Studio

In 1898, the year after the loss of *Vanderveld,* Hemy determined to continue with a floating studio along with the one at his home, Churchfields, so he purchased a larger and much more substantial craft, converting her as before, but with many improvements. He called her the *Vandermeer.* She is seen here moored beyond the fishing boats on the outside of Falmouth Custom House Quay. Trefusis Point is seen across the waters behind her.

Studio Interior at Churchfields

In what can only be viewed as presenting a stark contrast to the workrooms created on the two boats, the interior here is of Charles Napier Hemy's home base studio in Churchfields. This no doubt provided a suitable atmosphere in which to impress visiting dealers of the importance of his work, his standing as a Royal Academician, and the value he placed on his canvases which were fetching as much as a thousand pounds each – no small sum at the turn of the nineteenth century.

Naval Warships

Quite late in his career Napier Hemy worked up an interest in the Naval Ships that were often to be seen in Falmouth waters prior to World War One. The home fleet had taken to carrying out exercises between Ushant in France, Scilly and Fastnet, coming into Mounts Bay and Falmouth to lay up in between. This photograph taken from a cruiser in Falmouth Bay, might well have been used by the Artist, along with the sketches he made on board, for reference in his painting titled 'Warships Manoeuvering'. The Anti-Torpedo chain curtain is clearly shown here secured along the vessels deck side.

Wood Lane Falmouth 1890s

Henry Scott Tuke came to live in Falmouth with his parents in 1860 in a house at the western end of Wood Lane when he was two years old. They moved from there once and then back again before he enterered the Slade School of Art in London on January 25th 1875, Today he could have walked across the road to

Falmouth School of Art which now almost monopolises one side of the street. In 1883 he went to live in Newlyn and was very active for a short while with the Newlyn School painters, but returned to Falmouth in late 1885. Here he was to spend most of the rest of his painting life. Like Charles Napier Hemy he bought a boat to turn into a studio, the 'Julie of Nantes' an old French sailing vessel and moored her at Greenbank, Falmouth, where he painted many of his best known canvases.

Henry Scott Tuke's Studio, Falmouth

TRANSPORT UP AND DOWN

Although numerous histories with supporting photographs have now covered so fully the activities and development of the Great Western Railway throughout the county, no general compilation of Cornish images would seem complete to me without the inclusion of some visual reference to its existence and service to the life of the people here for over a century. Adding then to the photographs in my previous book, are those selected here, with the hope that several may be new to aficionados of railway history.

Ponsandane Wooden Viaduct, 1904

Seen here, the train pulled by the 3400 Bulldog Class Locomotive, 'Paddington' having traversed the county, passing over some of the finest of Brunel bridges, completes her journey around the bay and into Penzance main terminus station over this wooden viaduct. It is not difficult to imagine the conditions encountered on arriving in a south-easterly gale whipping up heavy seas.

**Duke Class
Locomotive, 'Amias'**

This gives a further splendidly dramatic close up of a goods train on the Ponsandane wooden viaduct.

Locomotive 7925, 'The Cornishman' Express

Stan Harris of Penzance who recently retired as a driver of mainline passenger diesel locomotives, began life on the railway as a fireman, and in 1961 and 1962 during those last days of steam he often worked on the footplate of 'The Cornishman' Express. It was his responsibility to fire her up between Penzance and Exeter and to calculate the amount of fuel required to see her out of the county. When I questioned him on this point, he said that between Penzance and Plymouth he would stoke her with a minimum of two and a half tons of best steam coal by hand. No wonder stokers were known for being thirsty men! This is the down train waiting at Camborne station.

Penzance Station, 1950s

Cedric Appleby of St Erth, a great enthusiast of Cornish railway history, took this excellent photograph of Penzance Station whilst still a youth using a simple Kodak camera. This was in the last decade of steam when the three tallest buildings then seen on the town skyline are as shown here, from left to right: St Mary's Church, the Gasworks and the dome of the Market House.

View Over Penzance Station

I am not sure how this low aerial photograph was taken, or who made it, as it was not acknowledged, but together with Cedric's photograph seen above, it does nicely complete the picture of the station layout in relation to the rest of the town.

Longrock Servicing Sidings

Locomotive 6911 'Holker Hall' waiting on the coal shed at Longrock servicing area between Penzance and Marazion.

**Track Work
Near St Erth**

This saddle tank locomotive is located, as far as can be established, waiting with her truckload on the gradient as the main line from Penzance approaches St Erth Station. Work is in progress laying, or relaying the second track.

ST ERTH TO ST IVES BRANCHLINE

Diesel locomotives have now replaced the little pannier tank locomotives that once added that extra magic of steam travel to the sounds, sights and smells of this short, but unique coastal journey. The journey along the Lelant estuary animated by sea birds and their calls, the almost white sands and blue of the summer sea in St Ives Bay, or in contrast, its sometimes steely indigo in stormy weather, remain unforgettable experiences.

St Ives Station

Looking towards the Island, with Porthminster Beach below.

Looking South-east from St Ives Station

Carbis Bay Station

The branchline to St Ives was the last in the county to be built using GWR broad gauge and opened on 1 June 1877. On the return journey to St Erth three station stops are made at Carbis Bay, Lelant Saltings and Lelant.

This shows a halt during a return journey to St Erth. The station building and ticket office are above the track left.

Redruth Station

Some years ago, whilst on a rail journey, I made an observational remark to a fellow traveller during the halt at Redruth regarding the large number of iron spike-top railings surrounding the station. It seems, so he told me, that when the Great Western Railway Company eventually arrived this far west, bringing civilization to the people, they took away all the spears of the Cornish and used them as perimeter defences throughout the county. Certainly a lot of them had found their way to Redruth. I was however rather inclined to take this explanation with a pinch of salt such as that used to cheer up the sausage roll I purchased in the British Rail cafeteria on arrival at my destination, Truro.

Truro City Station

Taken in the early 1900s this shows a Bulldog Class locomotive pulling the down train for Penzance taking on water.

Carharrack

The Redruth and Chacewater railway opened on the 30 January 1826. At first this 4ft-gauge mineral line ran for nine miles from a summit point near to Redruth via Lanner, relying on gravity for the down journey to Restronguet Creek and Point Quay on the Fal River. Horses were then used to pull the trucks back up again. It was added to with branchlines in various directions to serve the requirements of some of the richest copper mines in the area. This is a rare view of one of these lines on the outskirts of Carharrack Village, showing a gate entry off the main track. Tin and copper ore was taken down to the docks where the discharged trucks were loaded with coal and other necessities for the return journey. In 1854 two 0-4-2 tank locomotives were acquired to further this work, appropriately named 'Miner' and 'Smelter', but horses continued to be used also. After difficulties set in with the general decline in mining during the last years of the nineteenth century, the line was eventually forced to close on the 25 September 1915. Today a few road names in this village give the only clue to its once busy existence, except amazingly, when I made a brief tour of the immediate surrounding lanes, there up a hill on the way out, in the locality this photograph was taken, I came across an old rusting iron bridge, once part of it.

The Great 'Contractors Locomotive' Mystery

The only clue I have to offer the viewer of this photograph is that it came with a small group of prints and glass plates, some of which were positively identifiable as mid Cornwall. Both locomotives I'm fairly certain are contractors' engines and it's probable that ballast is being carried in the top trucks. The man standing centre has got to be the gaffer. Is it depicting track laying. All suggestions will be gratefully received. It's just one of those railway prints I felt I couldn't leave out as it poses so much interest and surely someone out there will know all about it.

Portreath Harbour

In mid Victorian and Edwardian times Portreath Harbour with its Hayle Railway branchline and further branch connection to the main line North Pool sidings, made it one of the most important small ports in West Cornwall for the shipping out of ore from the mines, and as a reception port for coal. An extensive rail layout for holding trucks was always busy, as the first of these two photographs shows. The first also features the long rope-worked incline up which the trucks were pulled to the clifftop, prior to being hitched to a steam locomotive for their journey to Hayle. By the beginning of the 1930s however much of the traffic in and out had finished, and by the middle of the twentieth century only a trickle of coasters and small colliers visited the harbour. Now a housing complex covers the centre area where the wagons and service buildings stand.

Coal Trucks, Portreath Harbour

Great Western Bus, Penzance, 1903

The first GWR bus service in Cornwall was that opened by the company on 17 August 1903 with a twenty-two seater Milnes-Daimler motor vehicle. This further conveyed passengers leaving the branchline train at Helston station on as far as The Lizard and surrounding district. The company having obtained authorisation orders to develop light railway branches from their main line at places throughout the county during the early 1900s, switched a number of these over to road bus routes, quite often saving construction difficulties and the associated expense, or just because it seemed a better business decision to answer a particular service requirement.

This photograph taken outside Penzance station was made, as far as can be established, on the day the first bus from Penzance to Marazion was put into service, 31 November 1903. The vehicle is another 16hp Milnes-Daimler. By the late 1920s the GWR buses were conveying over eight million passengers around the county in a year. 1929 saw the Western National Company take over all this business in Cornwall and much of the West Country.

First Flight Preparations, Poniou Meadow, Penzance, 1910

As so often happens the very image that would complete the picture of an event eludes all efforts at discovery until after the story's been published. I refer to the early aviation photograph featured in my previous book, *Lost Cornwall*, which showed Claude Grahame-White making the first ever historic flight in Cornwall over Penzance on the evening of the 23 July 1910, captured by the local photographer Vaughan T Paul. Hardly had that book come off the press than this rare view from an unknown amateur's camera of the evening preparations for that flight was presented for my interest by an enthusiast friend, Michael Eddy of Penzance. Faded and dog-eared but still with its detail intact I was able to realize this print after carefully copying it. Gusting winds had all day hampered attempts to prepare the Farman biplane until around 6pm when the weather was considered suitable for the necessary preparations for flight to begin in front of the gathered spectators who had paid 2 shillings and 6 pence for the privilege.

Gustav Hamel's Bleriot at Trengwainton, 1913

Yet another snapshot discovery, this time of preparations on the 4 September 1913, at Trengwainton, near Penzance, when Gustav Hamel came to fly his Bleriot aircraft over the town and surrounding countryside.

Left: **Gustav Hamel About to Take off at Trengwainton**

Below: **Over Trengwainton Fields. 4 September 1913**

Here Hamel in his Bleriot appears to hang almost suspended over the grounds of Major Bolitho's Trengwainton Estate fields, like some giant dragonfly.

Henri Salmet, at Penzance, April 1914

Fortunately for Henry Salmet, he had had his aircraft fitted with a float undercarriage at Falmouth after a previous spot of bother whilst attempting a landing on Gyllngvase beach. When further problems ensued after he set off for Penzance on 27 April and was forced to land in a choppy sea, it was possible to tow him round The Lizard and into Mount's Bay, as seen in this rare photograph, and eventually to the safety of Penzance floating dock.

THE CIRCUS COMES TO TOWN

The First Car in Penzance c.1900

I refuse to be firm about the date of this event except to say that several mentions of it I have come across put it between 1898–1902. I know for sure the car was shown off in Penzance during a visit to the town by what was then a circus, but soon to become a fairground concern, eventually as Anderton & Rowlands, well known throughout the whole of the twentieth century in the West Country.

The First Bus to London, 1919

This was the first bus, a Leyland, about to set off on the amazing journey from Penzance all the way to the 'big city' of London on 30 September 1919.

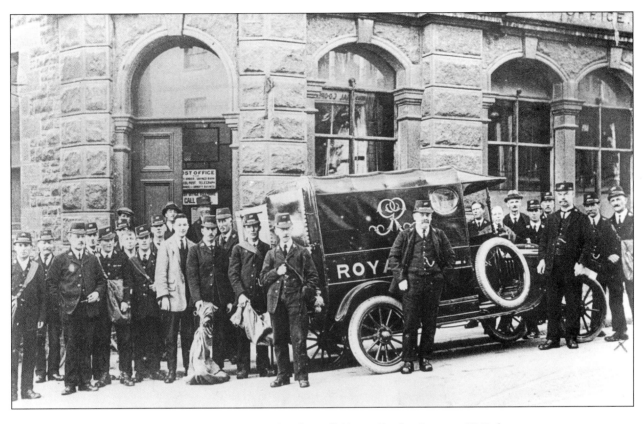

Penzance. First Motorised Mail Van. Early George V Reign

At least five pocket watch chains can be seen in this very official gathering outside Penzance main post office, emphasizing that the need for time-keeping. The mail getting through was paramount as everyone gathers around the new motorized addition to the mail delivery.

Wadebridge Jersey-cars c.1900

Jersey-cars were the horse-drawn forerunners of the motor-driven charabanc coach, and were sometimes referred to as such since they also fitted the French origin for the name: a long open carriage with transverse benches, or any carriage with several benches. This splendidly animated photograph, taken in Wadebridge at the junction of Molesworth Street and the Platt, around the turn of the nineteenth century, outside the Commercial Hotel (now the Swan Inn) has yet to reveal its secrets. Two Jersey-cars, lots of local interest, uniformed officers up front and other ranks spilling over the edges of the vehicles, even the maids have stopped work to view things. I have not identified the uniforms and service they represent but a military historian may well accomplish this immediately. The uniforms look to be made of the twill fabric serge, used I've noted for sailors' outfits, whilst all but one of the men present are sporting moustaches of a Russian or Polish fashion of the time.

I have visited the town recently, contacted various people and archives, ordered a pint of beer in the bar below the window the maid is leaning out of, but so far I cannot enlighten the reader further. And whilst there are no prizes for coming up with the correct information, I've found from experience that someone somewhere out there knows exactly what it's all about. The trick to achieving a solution sometimes is to give the wrong information and then one is sure to ferret out that very person waiting with a correction immediately on publication. All contributions to the mystery will be gratefully received.

Man the Lifeboat!

Visual records of stormy seas and shipwrecks made using the camera are quite rare in the early years of photography, before the 1880s. Photographic emulsions were still quite slow and required good lighting if the short exposures necessary for success with the subject were to be achieved, a feature of the weather not often found during dramatic moments at sea.

Stormy Sea, Penzance Promenade

A lapse-time shutter speed has been used to capture this stormy sea, the result of a south-easterly gale blowing in from Mount's Bay. In this case it could well have been three to four seconds, heightening the visual effect as the white seas broke over the promenade, the extended exposure freezing its total form.

***Elizabeth and Blanche* Lifeboat**

I have selected this photograph with its wonderful sense of movement as the Penzance Lifeboat, the *Elizabeth and Blanch*, under the direction of the coxswain, thrusts out to sea, for it seems to symbolize and sum up in one picture the full commitment and heroic resolve demonstrated throughout history by RNLI crews everywhere. This launch to a rescue was taking place during the years of her move to Newlyn (1908–1913). Alfred Vingoe was coxswain until 1910 when T E Vingoe took over command.

Penzance Lifeboat *Richard Lewis*

This two ton self-righting lifeboat, stationed at the Wherry Town end of Penzance Promenade next to coast-guard houses, was considered the first really effective vessel to be stationed in the area. Previous boats had not been large enough for the conditions faced around this Cornish coastline or up to the valour of the crews who manned them.

The *Richard Lewis* was in service from 1865 until 1884. Tom Carbis, seen standing in the bow, was her coxswain for the whole time, the second coxswain, Higgins, is at the stern holding the tiller and chief officer Blackmore is the man standing with the bowler-type hat on the right. The boat had been donated by a Mr J. Chamberlain of Birmingham.

Newquay Lifeboat

In the early 1900s a crowd has gathered to watch a launching at Newquay. This may have been a demon-stration launch, however lifeboats along the whole length of the hazardous north Cornish coast have always had a demanding time answering the distress calls of shipping. In 1859 there were only four lifeboats in the whole of the county, based at Penzance, Sennen Cove, Padstow and Bude, with one station on the Isles of Scilly at St Mary's. Newquay soon added to this number by bringing a boat into service in 1861. During the seventy-three years until 1934 when a lifeboat operated from here sixty-two lives were saved. Since 1965 an inshore rescue boat is on callout.

St Ives Lifeboat, RNLI Registration No.765 – *Caroline Parsons*

Wherever a lifeboat is stationed, be it coastal town or village cove, a special local spirit of loyalty and enthusiasm to the cause of the RNLI service prevails, well demonstrated here as everyone on hand pulls the *Caroline Parsons* along the St Ives harbour road back to the boathouse after her return from sea, sometime in her period of service from 1933-38. During those five years she had been responsible for saving 73 lives, but was herself to become a victim of the sea that last year whilst going to the rescue in January 1938 of the *Alba*, a motor vessel carrying coal from Barrie to Cita Vecchia, and which had come to grief on the St Ives Island rocks. In the course of taking men off the distressed vessel she was struck by a sea that rolled her over, throwing the crewmen and those *Alba* survivors secured into the sea, where fortunately they escaped drowning and scrambled ashore. But the lifeboat was smashed up and became a total wreck. Tragically, the relief boat that was to follow her the *John & Sarah Eliza Stych* on launching a year later, in 1939, to reports of a stricken vessel somewhere out in the bay, was driven by the appalling conditions up onto Beach Rock, Godrevy, where all but one of the lifeboat's crew perished. The only survivor, William Freeman, was the one volunteer taken on at the last moment prior to the launch to make up the eight man crew required. In spite of the grief experienced by the whole town, the great community resolve to provide rescue for those in peril at sea, saw a relief boat, the *Caroline Aver & William Maine* brought from Padstow. On station by the New Year of 1940 she was to continue in service at St Ives until 1948, and in numerous rescues saved 34 lives.

Lizzie R Wilce and Mary Barrow

This photograph of two sailing ships which went ashore on Porthminster Beach, St Ives, on the night of 7 January 1908 is taken from a lantern slide set I have part of showing Cornish wrecks. The remarkable series of events surrounding this drama are that both vessels had left Swansea with cargoes of coal just two days earlier with a four-hour gap between their departures. Arriving off St Ives Bay in heavy seas brought about by a north-westerly gale the *Lizzie Wilce* was blown ashore near the pier head, to be followed in a few hours by the *Mary Barrow* as she encountered similar difficulties.

The St Ives lifeboat men had a busy night, but fortunately all the crews were saved. The *Mary Barrow* was later refloated, but the *Lizzie Wilce* was only fit to be sold to Falmouth salvors. This picture, looking across the seine boats, though not quite so dramatic in composition as the one seen in my previous book, gives a clearer picture of the situation of both vessels.

Cadgwith Cove Lifeboat

Although by the year 1922 lifeboats powered by engines were beginning to be placed at several stations around the county, Cadgwith retained a pulling boat until 1941, the last of these being the *Herbert Sturmy,* shown here, which was for twelve oarsmen and fifteen crew in total. Cadgwith first went into service in 1867 and continued until 1963 during which years the men who manned her boats saved 388 lives.

Penzance Lifeboat, *Cape of Good Hope,* 1909

Older photographs of pulling lifeboats carrying out a rescue are quite rare to find since for both technical and other obvious reasons, the chances of a photographer being on hand or anywhere in the vicinity at the time to record the action were fairly remote. On 21 February 1909, the Yarmouth drifter *Renown* was caught close

inshore at low tide by the heavy seas of a southerly gale and forced in and up onto the flat rocks behind Penzance Albert Pier. On this occasion however a photographer was able to secure a vantage point on the harbour wall to give us this picture. The *Cape of Good Hope* was able to get a warp to the stricken vessel, attach this to a point on the pierhead of the south quay, and by this and other means the *Renown* was pulled free as the tide rose again.

St Anne, Porthleven, 1931

The way the photographer has organized the open expanse of light to contrast with the thrusting form of the stricken vessel, thus amplifying the drama taking place here on Porthleven beach, leads one to think this must be the work of an inspired professional. In fact the original I have for this copy is from a 127 film size contact print and was a snapshot, taken most probably with a vest pocket folding Kodak camera. The *St Anne* was driven ashore at Porthleven on 3 November 1931 in a south-westerly gale whilst on passage from Cardiff to Vannes in Brittany. Fortunately all the crewmen were rescued by breeches rocket line under the direction of one, Frank Strike. This is, as I've expressed before, one of those shipwreck images which like many others, engages one's senses because of its picturesque visual impact, but which I would immediately feel required other considerations regarding purposeful presentation if loss of life had also been a part of the event.

SS *Falmouth Castle*, 1919

Larger boats and ships are meant to be seen on the high seas. It's the strangeness of seeing a vessel of this size where it obviously shouldn't be and can't survive for long that always provokes interest. Seen here in March 1919 the *Falmouth Castle* was beached by her master in Porthcurno bay after she had struck the Lee Ore reef near the Runnel Stone rocks approximately two miles west. Once again all the crew were rescued by rocket line. She was in fact refloated later and put into service again.

St Mary's Lifeboat, *Elsie* c.1919

The first lifeboat on the Isles of Scilly, was that established on St Mary's in 1837. Until 1919 when the first motor-powered boat arrived, the *Elsie*, seen here, they were all pulling and sailing craft. In the 168 years to date, well over 500 lives have been saved. St Agnes also had a lifeboat in service from 1890, and in 30 years was responsible for saving 262 lives. It had to close in 1920, so I am told, due then to the difficulty of raising a crew from the reduced numbers of men available on this off-island.

Opposite page, top: **Sennen Cove Lifeboat c.1922**

The first lifeboat was established at Sennen Cove in 1853, it weighed one ton eight hundredweight, and cost one hundred and twenty five pounds. Its name is now not known for certain, but it was donated by the National Shipwreck Institution. Our photograph here is of the first motor-powered boat, the *Newbons*, which arrived at the cove for the first time in May 1922, here seen at the head of the slipway. Although motorized she was still fitted out with sails, a set of spars and oars, in case of an engine failure emergency. On 8 October 1923, she made the first of her many rescues when she went to the distressed SS *City of Westminster* saving 13 lives. She served this dangerous and difficult coastline off Land's End for 26 years until 1948. Her predecessor was called the *Anne Newbons*. She is actually in this picture, visible between the boathouse and the cottage, centre right.

Opposite page, botom: **Sennen Cove Lifeboat, Crew of the *Susan Ashley***

John Chope of Sennen Cove, a lifeboat crewman for 34 years and one of the longest serving members of the RNLI when he retired from the service in 1991, was immediately able to give me the names of this crew who had just returned from a rescue, possibly the saving of four men from the former War Department hulk, *Empire Flamingo,*on 26 October 1948

    The coxswain is John Roberts who took over the command that year. The names of the crew here are as follows, in order left to right: Alfred George, Henry Nicholas the engineer, Nathaniel George, Willie Trenary, John Roberts the coxswain, James Howard Nicholas, Dick Penrose, Charlie Trenary and E. George. The photograph was taken by a young news photographer, Harry Penhaul, affectionately referred to locally as Flash Harry.

Wreck off Cape Cornwall, 1932

The only cape in Great Britain lies approximately three miles north of Land's End. Winter storms are often followed by days of thick fog, and over the centuries countless vessels have come to grief around these cliffs and headlands. This is the 2082 ton SS *Glamorgan Coast* well wedged in on the rocky cove to the side of Cape Cornwall on 13 September 1932.

SS *Glamorgan Coast* – Eyeing Up the Wreck

Its recorded her cargo was salvaged, but its not certain by whom! There is certain to be a good percentage of St Just locals eyeing up the possibilities in the gathered crowd seen here.

The *Baltic*, from Ireland, 1907

Even in sea dramas there is sometimes the proverbial silver lining to be witnessed. When, on the night of Friday 1 November 1907, the *Baltic*, a Thames sailing barge making for Newlyn harbour was caught in the a south-easterly gale and in the poor visibility ran up on to Mousehole Island, it was to present considerable rescue problems. But it was also to bring romance into the village with it. The Penzance lifeboat the *Elizabeth and Blanche*, summoned to the vessel's distress, found that due to the low tide in her Penzance berth that she couldn't launch, the wheels of the lifeboat carriage stuck fast in the harbour mud. Mousehole men with great resolve decided to hoist a fishing boat, the *Lady White,* up and over the heavy timber baulks used for blocking off the harbour mouth in winter from the worst excesses of the gales, and attempt a rescue in this manner. This they successfully achieved and all the crew of the stricken boat were taken off. One of the men from the *Baltic* however, Adam Torrie, stayed on in the village after the others had gone home having fallen in love with the Harbour Master's daughter whom he went on to marry. This photograph was obviously taken a short time after the event as the postcard seen next tells us.

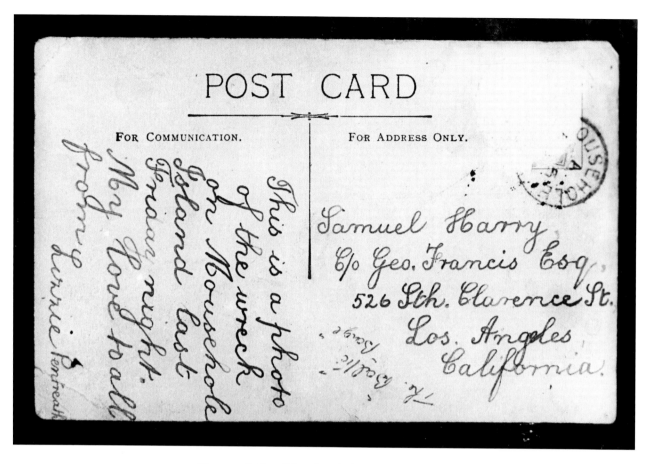

News of the Wreck of the *Baltic*, 1907

This postcard had travelled all the way to Calfornia from Lizzie Pentreath in Mousehole, informing Samuel Harry of the event, and maybe it was Samuel who brought it all the way back again when he returned perhaps to marry Lizzie (well somebody brought it home again!). It would be nice to think it worked out that way.

MID WEST AND SOUTH CORNWALL

For the purpose of presenting this part of the collection, I am loosely drawing a line from the south coast to the north across the county just west below Camborne, and taking in the countryside to another division just north and east of St Austell.

Trelowarne Street, Camborne c.1905

This photograph was taken around 1905 at the west end of this street near to the terminus of the only public transport tramway in Cornwall which linked Camborne to Redruth. The service opened on 7 November 1902 and was immediately a great success carrying over one million people in its first year of operation.

Tuckingmill, 1904

Pendarves Street, between Camborne and Redruth, 1904. The tall pole supports used to carry the electric power cables for the trams are still in place, used today for street lighting.

Dolcoath Mine, Camborne, 1903

This view of Dolcoath, one of the most important of Cornish mines, we know was taken after 1897 as it shows the new colliery head-frames erected that year by Holmans the major mining engineers in Cornwall, while smoke pours from the chimney stack of a newly built and bigger compressor hall shed. I have yet to find out the occasion for this gathering of miners for the photograph.

The Gig at Dolcoath

In my previous book, *Lost Cornwall,* I included a number of photographs from the 1894 publication by the Camborne photographer J C Burrow FGS, ARPS, which was published with actual photographic prints stuck into the book. This was made possible as the late George Burrow of Hayle, grandson of the author-photographer, became a good friend and allowed me to make copy negatives from the originals, three further examples are included here from this source. The man engine shown previously allowed a number of men to move up and down the levels at the same time. This gig however, holding just a couple of miners, was used for quick descent or return to the surface.

The Bottom of Cook's Kitchen Engine Shaft

In another part of the Herbert Thomas article referred to elsewhere, he writes 'The fantastic shapes of some of the rocks are shown up, and in the strong light (he is speaking of photographic flash powder and acetylene light) with hollows in deep shadow, it is easy to imagine one sees colossal heads of human beings or other animals. It is a pity one cannot photograph the boom that shudders through the mine when a blast takes place'.

A Mill at the 412 Fathom Level

The heat below ground at depths like this could be intense, and miners often worked stripped to the waist. It also presented problems for J C Burrow when taking the photographs for '*Mongst Mines and Miners*, due very much to its effect on the plate emulsions, camera lenses and flash powder used. In an article by Herbert Thomas, titled 'Peeps Through a Camera Underground' published in 1896, the author gives some idea of the problems encountered by Burrow. He writes 'I can write the more appreciatively from having spent a day with Mr Burrow in the bottom of Dolcoath, when he was making his first attempts and scoring ten failures for every success. My enthusiasm evaporated at the end of the day, but Mr Burrow's was only beginning to rise and after a score or more subsequent struggles he has produced a book of mining photographs of the highest interest and value'.

**Gould's Engine,
Wheal Grenville Mine**

South Crofty Mine

Heroic, majestic, awe inspiring, titanesque, one could continue to add adjectives to this list to anchor one's feelings to when viewing these and other nineteenth century Cornish mine workings. The South Crofty engine house with its well defined granite walls and chimney structure which has a finished brickwork top, seems fully to fit the descriptive title 'Cornish Cathedrals' which these unique industrial buildings have gained over the century since they stopped working.

Bowling Green, Helston c.1900

A line followed in a south-westerly direction from Camborne brings us to Helston. One of its finest features is the bowling green, well photographed by the fine Falmouth-based photographer, W M Harrison at the end of the nineteenth century.

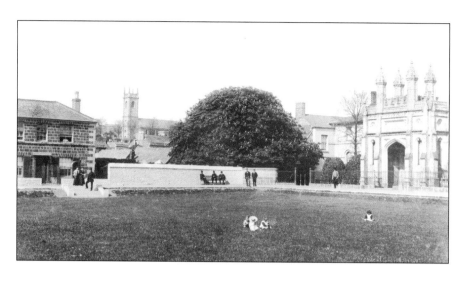

Helston 1890s

Helston was always busy in the nineteenth century as a link town between Camborne and Falmouth, Penzance and Falmouth, together with other cross routes including those established to serve the growing tourism seeking the delights of The Lizard peninsula. This print, the only one in my collection of the subject, though of poor quality, does show Blackwell's Angel Hotel which was a major centre in the town for the posting trade. It is just possible in the original glass plate negative to make out that the nearest vehicle is the Helston-to-Lizard horse bus.

Porthleven c.1900

The old Loe Bar road west out of Helston took one to Porthleven fishing village, as it does today, only then the housing estates and bungalows that now predominate along the journey were absent, leaving one free to enjoy this uncluttered coastal view. In the foreground is Mr Searle's Farm, while the tearooms that were run by a Mr Pascoe are on the left of the road near the cliff edge.

Cadgwith Cove Cottages

Cadgwith Cove seen here around the turn of the nineteenth century is just east of Lizard Point, and like other coves on this exposed coastline the cottages huddle close under the hillside for protection against the worst excesses of the southerly ,and south-westerly winter storms.

Lower Market Street, Penryn c.1900

North-easterly, from Cadgwith, crossing the King Harry Ferry we come to Penryn. In the early Middle Ages, Penryn along with Mousehole had importance as a port destination for pilgrims en route from Launceston through the county on the Royal Cornish Way as it was known. Here they embarked on ships which would take them to Spain. Its history is rich in detail, for instance both the Spanish and the French tried attacks on the town in Tudor times. In the following centuries it was a hive of activity, with woollen, flour and paper mills, merchants for fish exporting, whilst quarrying and quarry-stone shipping under the ownership and direction of John Freeman & Son became a major industry in the nineteenth century. This family came to own and work granite quarrying in much of Cornwall, supplying stone to a Victorian Britain busily engaged in building and engineering work everywhere, both at home and abroad.

Oyster Dredger c.1900

The oyster dredger shown here about 1900 is moving up the Fal estuary to the fisheries in one of the creeks that lead off from the river before it reaches Truro. A sailing dredger will look very much the same today, as a local by-law prohibits the use of motor vessels or any other motive power for this fishing. This makes both the boat and the surviving fishing method unique.

Market Street, St Day c.1900

This wide street with an unusual clock tower imparts an almost northern Italian feel. Its life was very much bound up in the nineteenth century with the mining that went on around, with the United Mines being the most important as well as one of the most difficult and demanding to work. It is said that in the deepest levels men had to work in temperatures of 115° Fahrenheit, with air so bad in some places it was difficult to keep the candles they were working by alight. Where water was present it was often hot enough to be scalding.

Redruth 1907–08

A revival in the Cornish mining industry during the middle Edwardian years gave both Camborne and Redruth a much needed injection of prosperity which this busy main street scene seems to reflect.

Truro c.1890

This view across the city shows clearly the architect J L Pearson's partly completed Cathedral sometime after 1887 by which time two bays of the nave were completed. Following this it was not until 1899 that further construction work of real importance was continued. Brunel's wooden viaduct is still clearly visible on the far right of the Cathedral, to be replaced at the beginning of the 1900s with the magnificent stone viaduct seen there today, opened officially on 14 February 1903. Truro had been a port since medieval times though by the late nineteenth century, when this photograph was made, much of its former trade had gone to Falmouth, and its Custom House was closed in 1882. As can be seen however, good sized ships were still sailing right upriver and into the centre of the city to discharge their cargo, or take on exports.

Truro Cathedral From St Mary's Street c.1910

Celebrations marking the completion of all the major work on the Cathedral took place in June 1910, the two western towers were finished that year. This photograph could have been taken then, if not, certainly within a short time after.

Bank Building, Truro

Designed by the Redruth architect James Hicks in the 1880s, this bank combines a number of the fashionable ideas regarding the use of ornamental application to impart importance to buildings that was such a feature of the late Victorian and Edwardian periods. Construction ideas based on the Gothic Revival, Continental Baroque, Arts and Crafts movement, Italian Renaissance, and a number of other sources were all applied freely. Hicks was to some extent not unlike Silvanus Trevail FRIBA who was responsible for a number of Truro's major buildings, and may have been partly influenced by him. The building is now the main premises of Barclays Bank in the city.

Cathedral Lane, Truro, 1905

Truro Hospital Interiors c.1900

These three interior photographs are from glass quarter-plate negatives I purchased locally some years ago. They provide a rare glimpse of hospital ward environment in Edwardian days. On the packet which contained them was simply written, Truro Hospital, so this I have assumed to mean the City Hospital. It is not often one finds old photographed interiors like this, because few people would take a camera to record a hospital interior, or be allowed to, especially at the beginning of the twentieth century when these images were made. The added problems of having to use only the available light, plus the slow shutter speed required, is evident in the last of these images as the nurse moves towards the child. There's no television to watch but certainly plenty of pictures and prints, together with suitably uplifting texts.

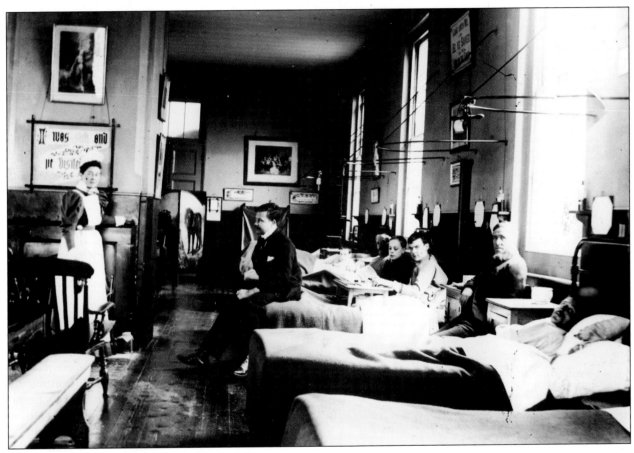

'I was sick and he visited me'. Above the fireplace behind the nurse.

Ready for Matron's inspection.

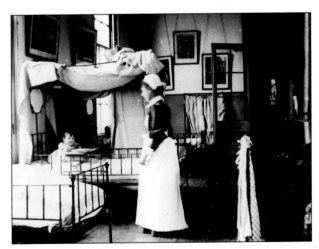

Children's ward.

St Mawes, 1890s

Located approximately fifteen miles south of Truro on the end of the Roseland peninsula, the village street seen here in the late 1890s had only just begun to be invaded on any scale by the yachting fraternity, and was, like Cadgwith, simply another of the many fishing villages found tucked into coves and bay inlets along the Cornish coast. The mainly serpentine stonework of the buildings, from local sources, is noticeably different from that of the open cut granite of many Cornish cottages, whilst the magnificent squared-off chimney constructions are a unique feature mostly of those areas in the county where serpentine prevailed as the building material.

Robarte's Road, St Dennis, 1930s

St Dennis is in the heart of the clay-mining country and this street is very similar to others, built to provide the clay workers with homes, in adjacent settlements. Their uniformity and general layout poses a marked contrast in a number of ways, with the coves and villages found throughout much of the rest of the county and there are strong references in them to the mining villages established in South Wales.

Clay Country Miners c.1910

Before the present high mechanization of the industry, the miners working life was an exactingly hard one as he shovelled the sand and gravel separated from the milky pooled china clay into wagons to be hauled up and deposited on the top of the ever-growing tips. Up to twelve tons a day of this waste was shifted by each man in a team like this one, posed here during croust break. In the days when Cornish wrestling was much more popular and widely practiced, they provided many of the champions of Cornwall. As with the tin miners, a boy seems always to have been a necessary part of the work gang to provide them with a 'gofore'.

China Clay Pit, St Austell District c.1900

This is a contact print from a half-plate I own which came with several other plates of the Roche district. I feel it may well be a view of workings as they were in the first half of the 1900s at Hensbarrow Downs, or those to the east of the road that links Stenalees with Roche. Incline tracks and sand drags are clearly visible on two of the dump hills and the winch house is seen on the left. Its exact location however is not important here, as it serves to represent the many extensive and awe inspiring sites like it to be found throughout the region. William Cookworthy could surely have had no idea that his discovery of Kaoling (China Clay as

we have called it) near Penzance in 1755 and soon after over a wide area in the St Austell district, was to change forever a large part of rural middle Cornwall into an industrial tip on a gigantic scale, with newly created communities whose lives became reliant on and wholly centred around the quest for this white gold. Although I have mentioned things in a little more detail with the support captions for photographs in my previous book, the extensive and fascinating history that surrounds the clay country development would easily fill a number of volumes. A visit to Wheal Martyn China Clay Heritage Centre at Carthew, near St Austell is a good starting point.

The *Kathleen & May*, Par Dock c.1950

Launched in 1900 at Connah's Quay, named originally as the *Lizzie May* and Irish owned, she was later renamed the *Kathleen & May* by a new owner and based at Bideford in North Devon. She was to become well known as one of the last of the wooden-built sailing coasters, carrying clay from Par Docks for the Irish and Stoke-on-Trent potteries, coal for Bristol, and a variety of other cargoes to ports around Britain. Her skipper for many years and the last to see her in regular service was Captain Tommy Jewell. She was still working , as far as I can establish, up to the early 1960s when she was taken to have preservation work done on her in Plymouth. It seems since then she was has been removed to London where further restoration has taken place and a 106 years after being built is still to be seen at moorings on the Thames.

In spite of the huge ranges of pits and white sand mountains that have swallowed up so much of the St Austell clay country, farming has continued tucked up deep valleys, between waste tips, on hillsides running up to the very edge of the engine houses, and in green meadows left around old and forgotten workings. This is Mrs Polly Jenkin about to milk her one cow on the family smallholding 'Evergreen Farm' at Carclew, having travelled all the way from Ballarat in Australia after she had married her husband there, Absolem Jenkin, a Cornishman by birth. Although a St Austell scene it reminds one much of type of subject chosen by the Newlyn School of artists.

Mevagissey c.1910

The name of this fishing village commemorates two Celtic saints, St Meva and St Issey. The Cornish word 'hag' meaning 'and' joins the two parts together. A fishing village with records going back to the building of a small quay in the 1550s and the inner pier in the 1770s, like St Ives and Newlyn it had an important pilchard fishing trade, supplying large quantities of the fish oil for London street lamps. Its also said that the fast-sailing Mevagissey luggers were the ideal craft to evade the watchful customs officers when smuggling activity made up for poor fishing periods. It's unlikely that much would get past the watchful eyes of this group of Mevagissey elders.

Fowey, 1890s

Looking upriver from St Catherine's Castle we can see what a fine sheltered anchorage was offered by the position of Fowey.

Polperro c.1900

This is taken from a photographic postcard and, long before digital imaging, it shows the publisher getting up to a little image manipulation as its now called. The Newlyn fisherwoman seen on the left was never in Polperro I'm quite certain, but is seen in exactly the same pose in a West Penwith card. Scissors or a sharp scalpel has been used instead of electronics to drop her into the composition.

Looe

Three photographs here, all of East Looe, once again show the narrow streets, inviting courtyards, sheltered corners and wonderfully varied and textured façades of the cottages, shops and inns, so typical once of the many old fishing villages and small towns around the Cornish coast. Now however, this is confined to a lesser number that have managed to escape, or at least deflect the excesses, of the tourist developer. Looe apart from having a very active fishing trade, became in the earlier nineteenth century a centre for the export of copper from inland mines and granite from quarrying, its development helped along with the construction and opening of the Liskeard-to-Looe canal in 1828.

Right: Looe, Fore Street and old house.

Below left: Back Street, Looe.

Below right: Bullers Arms, Fore street, old Looe.

MID, NORTH AND EAST CORNWALL

Bodmin Town

In the nineteenth century Bodmin was very much the county town, with Truro as the commercial and cultural capital. In 1838 the assizes were taken over from Launceston, Bodmin gaol was the major one in Cornwall, whilst it provided the Lunatic Asylum (as it was then called) and the Union Workhouse. In 1850 the recorded population was 3742, their thirsts being serviced by 15 public houses, with six lodging houses also to meet some of the needs of the crowds who always turned up for the public hangings, and the through coaches meant there was a lively posting trade. From the middle of the 1800s it was to become the garrison for the Duke of Cornwall's Light Infantry for a century, lasting to the middle of the 1900s. One would have thought that all this would have led to a good photographic record of things, but I can only say that in my forty years of collecting, I have found difficulty in coming across examples. Perhaps it is because in the second half of the nineteenth century only one local photographic business is mentioned, that located in Honey street, run first by William Henry Broad and then by Joseph his brother, with the business eventually going to one Arthur James who's photographic cards were always back-stamped Enterprise Studio, Honey and Turf street, Bodmin. Certainly the two shown here, taken in the early 1900s, present a lively buzzing picture of the town, but these are not by local photographers.

Fore Street, Bodmin 1906, looking east.

Looking west up Fore Street, Bodmin.

Dean Street, Liskeard c.1890

Liskeard has an elegance about it which is characterised by its late Georgian houses and hotels and stucco terraces. Even today, with all the motor vehicle through traffic, it still gives a visitor the feeling of being a traditional market town. The past that is reflected in its quietly grand architecture came about from the prosperity generated by the copper and lead mining industry in the area, particularly from the receipts when the workings on Caradon Hill at the edge of Bodmin Moor came good.

Old Houses, Church Street, Liskeard c.1900

An early 1900s photograph. Obviously a posed composition, but nonetheless pleasing for that.

Looking Up Church Street, Liskeard, 1890s

I have included this second view of the street. It shows Broad's Glass and China Warehouse. This would appear to be the earlier of the two views since the shop window looks Victorian, whilst the façade alteration in the previous print is Edwardian.

The Parade, Liskeard c.1893

This photograph is of The Parade and as far as I have been able to establish was taken around 1893. On the right is the Fountain Hotel and to the left of the centre road is Stones London Restaurant, whilst centre left the splendid Victorian drinking fountain stands surmounted by its gas lamp.

The Parade, Liskeard early 1900s

This more animated view, though not as well taken as the previous photograph, does show how fine and open a feature The Parade presented. On the extreme right can be seen a building with a portico. This was Webb's Hotel, built in 1833 and well established as the foremost in the town.

Fore Street, Callington c.1908

This shows Fore Street, Callington, east of Liskeard the town stands astride the Launceston-to-Plymouth road. The design of the bus seems to date the print at around 1908.

Cawsand

Sometimes referred to as forgotten Cornwall, the fishing cove village of Cawsand is tucked around a bay inlet from Plymouth Sound and is well off the main tourist route into the county, though it does provide a handy watering place for Plymothians. A tributary stream that runs down on the east side of Kingsand and Cawsand linking into the Tamar from the sea means you are in Cornwall one side and in Devon on the other. As at Porthgwarra at the other end of the county, featured earlier in this collection, the fishing here is very much a family affair, with one surname predominating, plus a couple of close friends. Here left-to-right (back row) we see Eric Marks, Harry Marks, then one man as yet not named, Algy Marks, with (front row) Hendra Cocks, centre Bill Cullis, and Billy Marks. The photograph was made around the 1930s, and as far as I can make out Cawsand continues to enjoy being forgotten during the season when much of the rest of Cornwall is heaving with visitors.

Port Issac c.1900

My collection of interesting photographic records of villages and towns on the upper North Cornish coast and on the A39, known as the Atlantic Highway, between Wadebridge and Bude on the Cornwall-Devon border is limited mostly to images from photographic postcards. Quite often unfortunately the quality of these mass-produced topographical records is flawed by poor detail and so I'm confined to selecting just the three that follow.

Located between Padstow and Tintagel, Port Isaac gets its name from from the old Cornish, Porth Izic, meaning corn port. It has a number of picturesque streets and the one shown here is so narrow it achieved the name of 'Squeezibelly Alley'. Its pier dates to the time of Henry VIII and its most prosperous past was when it was the major port for exporting slate from the nearby Delabole quarries. It acquired its first lifeboat in 1869, whilst fishing was suddenly given a welcome boost when the London & South Western Railway arrived in the later half of the nineteenth century and the fishermen were able to export catches directly to Exeter, London and Birmingham.

Camelford

We are looking approximately south-west up the main A39 through-road to Camelford Town Hall with its fine clock tower and weathervane. It is a small town with much history connected to legends of King Arthur, even in its name, which is linked by some to Camelot. Slaughter Bridge a mile up the Camel river is where Arthur's last battle is said to have been fought in the fifth century, and not far off on Bodmin Moor, is the stretch of water known as Dozmary Pool into which, legend has it, the sword Excalibur was thrown. There is another reference though to the town's name: in AD814, a King Egbert defeated the Cornish in the locality of 'Gafulford', and this may be the early origin of the present-day placename.

Tintagel Village Trevona.

Tintagel Village c.1900

Looking in an approximately westerly direction along the main street in Tintagel, the old Post Office on the left is often referred to as a fourteenth-century manor house, and then again by others to be a sixteenth-century farmhouse. Whichever it is the rest of the village is shrouded in legends of King Arthur so a little more mystery won't do any harm. It certainly looks different here from the village I saw one summer recently, for a start there's not a Merlin in sight, as there was one then standing by the Post Office in full magic regalia, smoking a cigarette and offering to tell fortunes. Plastic Excaliburs that lit up were being touted freely without any need for the tourist to visit Dozmary Pool. The church dedicated to its patron saint Matheriana is set apart on the headland just above the village, and has an almost fortress feel to it that can be quite awe-inspiring when viewed through a coastal mist.

Boscastle

Its name stems from the fortification that once existed here called Botreaux Castle. The Valency and Jordan rivers rush down steep-sided valleys into this harbour, constructed within the narrow inlet from the sea. Two stone quays break up the power of the winter storms are clearly shown here. Built to hold seas at bay, they also of course in the recent flooding drama helped along with other factors to restrict the outward flow out of the great flood waters.

Fishing once again was the main occupation and mainstay of the economy, but coasters also called here with coal for the mines and took away iron ore from Trebursye mines not far away.

Left: Towing a sailing barge into Boscastle

Below: View over Boscastle Harbour

Bude Haven c.1880

Harry, Samuel and Sarah Thorn were the professional photographers in Bude and have also to be considered amongst the best in the county. Sarah was the last to continue in the business and died at the age of 92 on 4 June 1932. They photographed many of the wrecks that fell foul of the hazards on this difficult and treacherous coastline (there is an excellent example of this in my previous published collection *Lost Cornwall*) whilst their visual records of the landscape and coastal scenery exhibit a great eye for composition and mastery of technique, as this print also demonstrates.

Torpoint

The Tamar River which creates a natural boundary between Cornwall and Devon, though crossed early on by fine bridges at Gunnislake and Launceston soon became too wide for a crossing to be attempted as it opened out towards Plymouth, that is until Brunel spanned it in 1859 with his magnificent Royal Albert Bridge. This carried Great Western Railway trains in and out of Cornwall. Ferry boats were used from earliest times from Torpoint and Saltash to cross to and from Plymouth, while the first steam ferry was built to make the crossing from Torpoint by James Meadows Rendel in 1834. The engine pulled what was virtually a floating bridge across by chains, and many marvelled at how you could get a whole team of horses on it still hitched to the carriage or wagon. Today's ferries are diesel driven and amongst the biggest in the world of their type.

This is Torpoint ferry sometime before 1907.

Fore Street, Torpoint, early 1900s.

The Crossing, Torpoint

AC 1125 must surely be amongst the first new-fangled petrol cars to use the ferry. No doubt someone somewhere will recognize great grandfather's pride and joy, or be able to tell by the registration exactly what date this was taken, so far this has eluded my research.

Saltash, 1903

Left: Tamar street, looking west about 1903.

Right: Tamar Street, Looking East, up to the Royal Albert Bridge.

The photograph on the right should perhaps be in a book on surrealism as well as in this collection to do it full justice. Did the photographer mean to pose the little girl at the end of the street so utterly alone under the all-encompassing structure of Brunel's gigantic railway bridge. However he managed the exposure, it certainly makes for a wonderful and original statement on the great engineer's achievement and represents I feel a photographic work of art.

 The bridge was opened on 2 May 1859 by Prince Albert and on 4 May that year the first rail traffic to Truro ran over it.

Launceston Market, 1906.

This is such a jolly, busy view of Launceston, the oldest entrance and exit gate into Cornwall that I have no intention of spoiling the ending of this collection by delving into the dark history of Robert of Montain's medieval castle, or the going's on in the towns notorious gaol which they shut down for good in 1829, long before photography. I would have been delighted to meet this scene on arriving into the county over the bridge from Devon!